WOMEN IN HISTORY

by
Jerry Aten

illustrated by
Kathryn Hyndman

Cover by Kathryn Hyndman

Copyright © Good Apple, Inc., 1986

GOOD APPLE, INC.
BOX 299
CARTHAGE, IL 62321

Copyright © Good Apple, Inc., 1986

ISBN No. 0-86653-344-3

Printing No. 9

GOOD APPLE, INC.
BOX 299
CARTHAGE, IL 62321

Pictures of several of the women are reproduced with permission from the *Dictionary of American Portraits,* published by Dover Publications, Inc., 1967, New York, New York. Edited by Rita Weiss, Everett Bleiler, Robert Hutchinson, Alan J. Marks, and Clarence C. Strowbridge.

TABLE OF CONTENTS

INTRODUCTION

From Sacagawea to Sally Ride, women in the United States have come a long way toward gaining equality in what was once a "man's world." But their gains have not been without effort. The perseverance and the courage of those who fought the battles and the achievements and accomplishments they've gained are all a part of the American story. While the forty women chosen for presentation in this book are by no means the only women who've brought the course of history to its present chapter, they represent a broad spectrum of avenues taken by women to be recognized in a "man's world."

The book was designed to provide a starting point for students who will want to get truly involved in research of the personalities and life-styles of their favorites. Each name presented begins with a brief one-page biographical sketch, including background information and the highlights of that person's trip into history. This is then followed by five thought questions based on an analysis of all that has been read. These questions should also provide an excellent starting point for a stimulating classroom discussion. Finally, there is a research question that can be used in a variety of ways. For those who become interested in the life of a particular woman who has made her mark in history, the question provides a starting point for further reading. The question may also be used as a research writing project. The bibliography in the back of the book should prove helpful to those seeking additional information and enrichment. The research question can also be used by teachers looking for an assignment to offer as an extra credit project.

The culmination of the study is Partners in Progress, a game for the entire class requiring recall of the important and the not-so-important facts and trivia that have been collected through the course of the study. There are forty game cards each containing five trivia questions. The correct answers are on the backs of the game cards. The format allows for the game's use by the entire class or as a competition between partners working in pairs. There are additional activities included that rely on the knowledge students have accumulated through the entire study. An answer key containing suggested responses to the questions is also included.

The number of women included makes the study an excellent ongoing project for the entire school year. Each woman can be highlighted for a few days, during which time students complete the reading and questions and participate in the class discussions. Research projects and additional readings can be assigned on occasion or as students find special interest. Perhaps a special section of the bulletin board can be set aside to present words and deeds and events that are most remembered about the woman being highlighted. The order of presentation in the book is alphabetical, merely for the sake of convenience in location, and does not suggest that they be assigned to students in that manner. Birth dates or events in history that can be tied to a particular woman may be a more appropriate method for determining order of presentation. Students will find some women more interesting to them than others, but enthusiasm on the part of the teacher will go a long way toward kindling that interest into a vocabulary study of some of the women who helped shape American history.

ABIGAIL ADAMS

Few women in history could match the influence of Abigail Adams in state affairs. As the wife of one President and the mother of another, she served in a very influential role during the infant years of the new nation. She exercised considerable political power in a wifely sort of way and was an early advocate of women's rights. Abigail was so skillful in the way she applied her influence that few even recognized the far-reaching implications. She would have publicly denied her power, because she had no desire for the limelight, but her sustained and brilliant correspondence to her husband during their long absences from one another have very definitely figured in the course of American history.

She was the daughter of a parson who would have preferred she had chosen to marry someone of the clergy in preference to a lawyer (John Adams), a profession not entirely respectable. It was during this time (pre-Revolution) that she became deeply involved in the politics of the day, listening for hours to conversations between John and his friends.

When the Revolutionary War was over, her husband was appointed Commissioner to France. There she learned the grace and charm that accompanied European culture traits that would prove valuable to her when she became First Lady. She was delighted when John was elected President after serving as Washington's Vice President for eight years. However, he had several political enemies and he was at times blunt and tactless, and his administration lasted only one term. Abigail was very bitter when it became evident that his main political rival, Thomas Jefferson, would probably win the election of 1800, and she was reluctant to move into the new President's House when the capital was changed to Washington, D.C. But being the trouper that she was and because she was very faithful to her husband's wishes, she did move, even though her stay was a short one. In fact she helped to launch society in the new capital by organizing the first full-dress reception to be held in the President's House, more popularly called the Palace. Saddened by the loss of the election of 1800 and by the loss of their son Charles, Abigail and John returned to their farm in Massachusetts. She always felt that history would vindicate her husband's decisions and it did. Seven years after her death, her son John Quincy became President of the United States.

Name _____

For Thinking and Discussing

1. In the midst of the advice she often gave to her husband John, Abigail once suggested that he ''remember the ladies and be more generous and favorable to them . . . .'' What was Abigail suggesting with this statement?

   _____

   _____

   _____

   _____

2. Why was the administration of John Adams an unpopular one?

   _____

   _____

   _____

   _____

3. Abigail herself was not a very popular First Lady, even though she did much to dignify the position. Why did some people criticize her action?

   _____

   _____

   _____

   _____

4. How did John Adam's tenure of duty representing the United States provide help to Abigail in her future role as First Lady?

   _____

   _____

   _____

   _____

Name _____

5. How did Abigail's influence help her son John Quincy to later become the sixth President of the United States?

_____

_____

_____

_____

_____

_____

_____

For Further Research

Look into the main differences between John Adams (of the Federalist) and his main political enemy Thomas Jefferson (who founded the Jeffersonian Democratic Party). Abigail Adams admired the views of both men.

JANE ADDAMS

The late 1800's saw the nation beginning to recognize the problems of big city slums and responding with reform measures. Jane Addams was one of those reformers who was a firm believer in what she called "Christian Humanitarianism" with men, women, and children joining in one family as God meant them to be. Considered both a rebel and radical, she shook up the political structure and made people aware of the social problems of her time. She ranks as one of the most influential women in American history.

The result of her "Christian Humanitarianism" was Hull House, a settlement in the crowded slums of Halstead Street in Chicago, Illinois. In the beginning it had no specific goals other than Jane Addams' basic philosophy, and the welcome mat was extended to all. Within a short period of time, however, certain recurring needs began to emerge that gave Hull House a personality all its own. Its location in the center of a factory and tenement area made it an ideal haven for the seven or eight "neighboring" nationalities of immigrants nearby, as well as people from all walks of religious communities. She fed the hungry, clothed the needy and brought medical care into their lives. She helped them to improve their homes and taught them arts and crafts. The presence of Miss Addams herself gave the place dignity and encouraged the establishment of other such settlements in major U.S. cities. Over 500,000 of Chicago's population at the time was foreign born and the 50,000 residents of Ward Nineteen (Hull House's location) were mostly immigrants who could not speak English.

Jane's quiet insistent demands of legislation to pass laws that would help the poor were heard, and the vision of Hull House expanded into other areas never before anticipated. The emphasis gradually shifted from scholarship to recreational interests, but the whole idea continued to be to make better, more well-adjusted citizens out of its patrons.

Jane Addams also helped to establish The Woman's Peace Party and was elected its national chairperson. Her strong position for peace jeopardized her Hull House and caused her to be expelled from the patriotic Daughters of the American Revolution. However, her participation in a peace-seeking mission to The Hague Congress of Women in 1915 brought about her vindication, as many of Woodrow Wilson's eventual recommendations for peace were based on her suggestions. She was awarded the Nobel Peace Prize for her efforts.

Name _____

For Thinking and Discussing

1. How did the fact that Jane Addams had considerable wealth contribute to the success of her Hull House?

   _____

   _____

   _____

   _____

2. What were some of the special interests and skills that were all a part of Hull House?

   _____

   _____

   _____

   _____

3. What was the secret of success for Jane Addams in making her program extend beyond merely seeking aid and assistance for those in need?

   _____

   _____

   _____

   _____

4. When Jane Addams was elected chairperson of the Women's International League for Peace and Freedom (earlier called The Woman's Peace Party), she risked the popularity of Hull House and was criticized by the American Legion as well as expelled from the Daughters of the American Revolution. Why were these groups critical of her stand?

   _____

   _____

   _____

   _____

Name _____

5. Jane Addams was often misunderstood and became the subject of much hatred and condemnation during her many years of work for social reform. What was the cause for these negative feelings by many people?

_____

_____

_____

_____

_____

_____

_____

For Further Research

Make note of some of the names of successful settlement houses all over the United States during the late 1800's as well as briefly noting some of the legislation and reform acts that were designed to help minorities and those living in slums.

LOUISA MAY ALCOTT

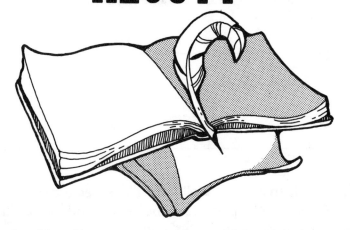

Louisa May Alcott grew up in a small New England town during the mid 1800's. Her father, Bronson Alcott, was a well-known educator whose ideas often lacked practicality and led to financial disaster. He felt that the Socratic method—that of questioning without forcing—was the way to educate all children. When his school failed, he moved his family to Concord where "Louy" grew up. She and her four sisters were very close, and though the Alcott family never had much money, her childhood experiences were happy ones.

She grew up in the company of such famous writers as Ralph Waldo Emerson, Oliver Wendell Holmes, Nathaniel Hawthorne, and Henry David Thoreau. Her first playhouses included diaries and dictionaries, which she had learned how to use before she was five. Her father constantly provided his daughters food for thought to stimulate their minds. As a child she read Shakespeare, Dante, Carlyle, and Goethe, which she borrowed from the libraries of the literary giants within her midst. She longed to be an actress, and she wanted to be a writer as well. Her early exposure to great literature and the minds of its creators created in her an independence in thought and deed that would carry over into her adult life. She developed some very strong feelings on politics and social reform. During the Civil War she served as a nurse and she lived alone in boarding houses, supporting herself as a seamstress and governess.

She wrote plays and stories in the attic, often working as long as fourteen hours a day! Her first successful book was entitled *Hospital Sketches* and she became editor of a magazine for young girls called *Merry's Museum* in 1868. At this point in her life she was an experienced storyteller and, at the urge of a publisher, wrote about her experiences as a child in a book she titled *Little Women.* She quickly penned the first part of the book and it became an immediate success. The second part soon followed and provided the financial security her family needed. Her charming story of the March (actually the Alcott) family was spiced with the gaiety of a Robin Hood ballad woven into the Concord scheme of life. *Little Men* and other novels for children followed. She later wrote novels for adults, but they were never as successful as those she wrote for children. In addition to her writing, she was active in the temperance movement and devoted her efforts to gaining voting rights for women.

Name _____

For Thinking and Discussing

1. How did the childhood experiences of Louisa May Alcott provide her background for her famous novel for children, *Little Women*?

   _____

   _____

   _____

   _____

2. Bronson Alcott, Louisa May's father, felt that every well-born child was a genius and that, if properly educated, that genius could be tapped. Describe his method for teaching children, a method that proved less than popular in Alcott's day.

   _____

   _____

   _____

   _____

3. How did Louisa May Alcott's exposure to such literary greats as Emerson and Thoreau help later in her career as a writer?

   _____

   _____

   _____

   _____

4. Louisa May Alcott developed a mind of her own at an early age and soon became actively involved in those causes which were most important to her. Briefly note some of her more important "crosses" to bear.

   _____

   _____

   _____

Name _____

5. How did her father, Bronson Alcott, help Louisa May in her pursuit of a career in writing?

_____

_____

_____

_____

_____

_____

_____

For Further Research

Find and read Louisa May Alcott's *Little Women.* Then compare and contrast the value system expressed with the value system of young women today.

MARIAN ANDERSON

The world famous conductor Arturo Toscanini once said of Marian Anderson, "A voice like hers comes once in a century!" This famous black contralto was born of a poor, but very close-knit family in south Philadelphia, Pennsylvania. All during her early childhood she was consciously aware of the rhythm in most sounds, be it the ticking of her father's watch, the passing click of a horse's hooves or the sound of her aunt singing her a song. She unconsciously absorbed other musical impressions from some of the simplest of scenes. Most of her early musical talent was performed in the church, where she became known as the "Baby Contralto." When she began to sing with the famous black tenor, Roland Hayes, she realized that she wanted to parlay her God-given talent into an actual living. Her own neighborhood began chipping in their nickels and dimes to support her professional lessons. She performed with the Philadelphia Choral Society, then won an appearance with the New York Philharmonic Orchestra by winning over 300 other contestants. But because of her race, she was denied the instant national recognition and acceptance her voice deserved. So she gathered together enough funds to get to Europe, where a number of famous musicians began to make favorable comments about her voice and poise. Her tour of Scandinavia really and truly escalated her to success; and during the next five years, she sang before packed houses all over Europe. She returned triumphantly to New York City in 1935 for a concert at Town Hall. So great was the success of this concert that she performed twice more before packed houses in Carnegie Hall.

She was capable of singing almost all forms of music, but she never once abandoned her love of spiritual singing and songs of Blacks which she had performed so well in her youth. Her whole career carried with it overtones of a tribute to her race, and she was proud to represent them well. One of the most moving of all her performances was before over 75,000 people at the Lincoln Memorial in Washington, D.C. In the shadow of the giant who had been so responsible for freeing her people, she sang in the evening sun with a voice that was perhaps even more beautiful and moving than it had ever been before. She was showered with honors and awards and received words of praise from powerful and influential people most of her adult life. Though a simple, sincere and humble person, she proved how great success can be to someone who dreams and works very hard to make those dreams come true.

Name _____

For Thinking and Discussing

1. At the age of three, Marian Anderson remembered being forced to sit in her high chair, which she did not want to do. At the height of her temper tantrum, she saw the flowers on the wallpaper actually start to dance. How could impressions like this as a child possibly help launch her on a career in music?

_____
_____
_____
_____

2. While enroute from her European tour to New York City, she lost her balance during a storm and fractured her foot. There was a question about whether or not she would be able to perform. She not only insisted that the show go on, but she refused to allow announcement of her injury. Why do you suppose she handled the injury in this manner?

_____
_____
_____

3. What incident in her youth "finalized" her burning desire for a career in music?

_____
_____
_____
_____

4. Marian Anderson closed many of her concerts with the spiritual "Crucifixion." In fact, even when she became famous, she continued to include spiritual music in her concerts. Why do you think this great contralto always seemed to return to the spiritual?

_____
_____
_____

Name _____

5. What was the occasion for Anderson presenting her concert in front of the Lincoln Memorial and how did it symbolize all that she hoped to represent?

_____

_____

_____

_____

_____

_____

_____

_____

For Further Research

Research from other sources the names of some of the influential artists and musicians who not only shaped the career of Marian Anderson but helped enhance its success with the things they said and the things they did.

SUSAN B. ANTHONY

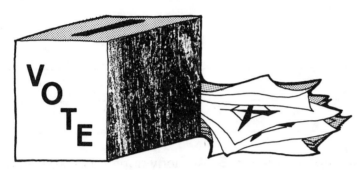

Susan Brownell Anthony was one of the true pioneers among women in their quest for equality among men. She helped to organize the suffrage movement and also was a firm believer in other major reform issues like temperance and antislavery.

She was born of Quaker parents in 1820 in Adams, Massachusetts. Her father believed strongly in education and organized a school in his house that was attended by Susan. She then taught school herself until she was recruited by Elizabeth Cady Stanton to lend her support to the movement for women. The two became associates and Anthony, convinced that she could never appeal to a man because of a cast in one eye, threw her heart and soul into the fight for equality. However, there was constant bickering and tension between the leaders, that included Anthony, Lucy Stone, Nette Brown and Stanton. During her campaign for temperance, she became even more aware of the prejudice against women and the low station in life they occupied. She pushed for women workers to organize into unions and following the Civil War began her fight for suffrage. The campaign began in Kansas where Anthony and her little troupe were often ridiculed, but some people did listen. In the end, however, suffrage was defeated in Kansas.

Susan B. Anthony refused to give up and in 1869 formed the National Woman Suffrage Association. She published a weekly tabloid-sized, 16-page paper called *The Revolution* that contained a variety of views about women and their needs for equality. The paper eventually lost $10,000, but Anthony paid off every penny of the debts through her lecture and personal austerity. A rival suffrage group organized under Lucy Stone, and the two groups waged their separate battles for equality for twenty years before finally merging. In 1872 she voted in the presidential election and was arrested and fined $100. Anthony never paid the fine and no further action was taken. In 1878 Senator A.A. Sargent introduced a woman suffrage amendment known as the Susan B. Anthony Amendment. It lingered on the desks of Congressmen for forty-two years before eventually becoming the nineteenth amendment in 1920. Anthony died in 1906, but the memory of her work will never be forgotten. In 1979 the government minted one-dollar coins bearing her resemblance, and she thus became the first woman so honored by having her picture on a coin in circulation.

Name _____

For Thinking and Discussing

1. Susan B. Anthony is well remembered as one of the real pioneers among women in their fight for equality. What were the areas of concern she challenged in various campaigns she waged through her entire life?

   _____

   _____

   _____

   _____

2. How was George Francis Train useful to Susan B. Anthony during their speaking tour in Kansas in 1867?

   _____

   _____

   _____

   _____

3. Why was there so much opposition when Susan B. Anthony and others took up the battle to win for women the right to vote?

   _____

   _____

   _____

4. In 1869 Susan B. Anthony and Elizabeth Cady Stanton formed the National Woman Suffrage Association. A rival group called the American Women Suffrage Association was formed by Lucy Stone and Julia Ward Howe. Why were there two such organizations when it would seem that a single united effort would have had more impact and effect?

   _____

   _____

   _____

   _____

Name _____

5. If she were still alive today, how do you think Susan B. Anthony would have reacted to the recent defeat of the Equal Rights Amendment?

_____

_____

_____

_____

_____

_____

_____

_____

For Further Research

It has been said that the antislavery movement and the movement for women's rights might have had different outcomes had they not both been in the public sentiment at the same time. Trace the history of both movements and discuss how the two, though different in goals, did much to help each other toward their eventual end results.

ELIZABETH BLACKWELL

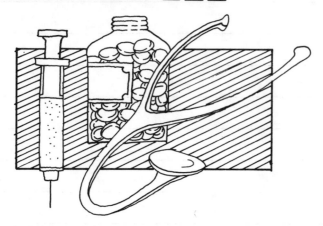

Elizabeth Blackwell became the first woman physician in the United States. To achieve this distinction, she overcame a great deal of personal ridicule and abuse by those who were against women doing anything beyond tending to their homes, their husbands and their children.

Born in Bristol, England, she emigrated to the United States when she was in her youth. She learned what she could about medicine from John Dickson, a clergyman doctor in Asheville, North Carolina. She later studied under his brother. After applying (and being turned down) to no less than twenty-nine different medical schools, including Harvard, Yale and all the schools in New York City, she was accepted for admission at Geneva College of Medicine (later a part of State University of New York in Syracuse) only after the men at the college had jokingly voted to accept her. Her first practical experience came in Philadelphia Hospital in 1848, where she helped combat an epidemic of typhus. She later wrote her thesis on the subject. She studied very hard and overshadowed her male counterparts, finishing at the head of her graduating class in 1849. Although penniless, she borrowed enough money to buy a black silk dress for the occasion because she felt it was important. She also refused to march in the graduation procession because she considered it unladylike.

Miss Blackwell continued her study of medicine abroad, then attempted to set up a practice in New York City. She was ostracized and discouraged wherever she went, but she did not give up. Eventually she bought a house in a New York City slum and opened a clinic with the help of a few New Yorkers, most of them Quakers. In 1857 she founded the New York Infirmary for Women and Children, and in 1867 she was able to add the Woman's Medical College. She spent most of her life championing the rights of women and in her later years, poured forth a great deal of effort toward gaining for women the right to vote.

In 1869 Miss Blackwell moved to London where she helped to establish the National Health Society of London and the London School of Medicine for Women. Among her writings are *The Physical Education of Girls* and *Pioneer Work in Opening the Medical Profession to Women*.

Name _____

For Thinking and Discussing

1. Elizabeth Blackwell was turned down by one medical school after another when she applied for admission. She was discouraged, but she didn't give up. What was there about her personality that forced her to continue looking?

_____

_____

_____

_____

2. She was a lady of determination and conviction. Once she was accepted into medical school, there was still a great deal of prejudice against her. Why was she subjected to such uncalled for ostracism?

_____

_____

_____

_____

3. When Elizabeth Blackwell did finally succeed in establishing her clinic, she built it in a slum area in New York City. Why do you suppose she chose a slum area?

_____

_____

_____

_____

4. Elizabeth Blackwell's crusade in her senior years centered around improving the rights of women. In fact she rode in a parade demonstrating for voting rights for women just a few months before her death. Why do you think she did this?

_____

_____

_____

_____

Name _____

5. Why do you think Miss Blackwell never married?

_____

_____

_____

_____

_____

_____

_____

_____

For Further Research

Find out where women are today in the medical profession. How many women doctors are there? What percentage of doctors are women?

PEARL BUCK

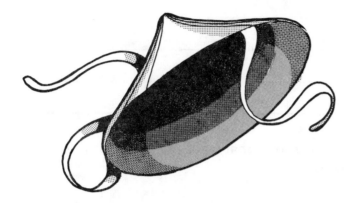

She was born Pearl Sydenstricker in Hillsboro, West Virginia, in 1892. She grew up in China, where her parents were missionaries. Although Pearl attended Randolph-Macon College in Virginia, before going to Europe at the age of seventeen, she returned to China shortly thereafter to teach. Before she ever began writing novels about China, she read all the Chinese novels she could find. This required the knowledge of between ten and twenty thousand Chinese characters as well as subjecting herself to an unconventional course of training, because Chinese novels of the day were considered vulgar and outside the standards of good literature. She also became familiar with the classics and was thus well-prepared when she actually began to write.

She married agricultural missionary Dr. John Lorring Buck and began teaching at the University of Nanking. Her marriage to Buck lasted until 1935 when she divorced him and married Richard John Walsh. Her first novel *East Wind: West Wind* was published in 1930. In 1931, she was awarded a Pulitzer prize for her book *The Good Earth,* an almost overnight best seller about the life struggles of Chinese peasants. In 1938 Pearl Buck was further honored by being selected as the recipient of the Nobel Prize for Literature for *The Good Earth* and other novels dealing with China. She was so overcome with the announcement that she thought a mistake had been made. Her trip to Sweden and graceful acceptance of the prize along with all the speeches and parties and press coverage made her extremely popular in Scandinavia. She became simply known as "The Pearl."

She preferred to be remembered for her books rather than herself, and the more than sixty-five novels plus hundreds of short stories and essays she wrote stand as a testament to her writing career. She also wrote about the contemporary American scene of her day, under the name of John Sedges, but she will always be better identified more famously with a Chinese setting. Her two autobiographical works were titled *My Several Worlds* (1954) and *A Bridge for Passing* (1964). Pearl Buck died in 1973.

Name _____

For Thinking and Discussing

1. How did Pearl Buck's childhood help her as an adult writer?

_____
_____
_____
_____

2. Describe the ten-year "apprenticeship" she served that made her a veteran writer almost overnight once she began writing novels.

_____
_____
_____
_____
_____

3. Pearl Buck had a most unusual education. Describe the various phases, both formal and informal, of the education of this amazing woman.

_____
_____
_____
_____

4. Why was her book *The Good Earth* an instant best seller?

_____
_____
_____
_____

Name _____

5. What was Pearl Buck's crowning achievement in life?

_____

_____

_____

_____

_____

_____

_____

_____

For Further Research

There is quite a story behind Pearl Buck's overwhelming reception by the people of Sweden when she went there to accept her Nobel Prize for Literature. Research the story and find out why she was so immensely popular.

JULIA CHILD

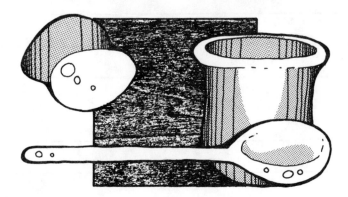

The name Julia Child became a household word during the 1960's when her popular television series on cooking called *The French Chef* aired on stations all over America. She started her adventures in cooking in Paris when her husband was stationed there with the foreign service. She studied at the famed Cordon Bleu and from there became interested in teaching others the art of French cooking. In 1961 she wrote *Mastering the Art of French Cooking.* It became a best-seller and her career was on its way.

She was born in Pasadena, California, in 1912, the daughter of a farm consultant. Because her parents were fairly wealthy, Julia seldom ever ventured into the kitchen as a child, preferring to be a tomboy. She grew to a height of six feet and wanted to become a basketball star at Smith College. After college, during World War II, she joined the OSS and was sent to Ceylon, where she met Paul Child, who would become her husband. He was a gastronome and Julia enrolled in a cooking school, determined to master the art of good cooking. When Paul was assigned to the American Embassy in Paris, she learned the French language and became interested in French cuisine. She met Simone Beck, who introduced her to the French way of doing things, and Louisette Bertolle, who had been planning to write a French cookbook. The three of them established L'Ecole des Trois Gourmandes, a French cooking school.

After getting the school well under way, the trio began writing their book. Finally in 1961 the book *Mastering the Art of French Cooking* was published. The book was an overnight success and was reviewed by critics as the finest volume on French cooking ever published. It led to interviews and talk show appearances, and during one such interview, Julia demonstrated on TV how to make an omelette. The response from viewers was overwhelming and *The French Chef* was born. It soon reached over one hundred educational stations nationally and was extremely popular. Her casual friendly approach without a prepared script added to the credibility and the show's popularity, and thousands of women (and men) became fans because she convinced them they could become good cooks, too. She also shopped personally for the ingredients, and almost ten hours of preparation went into each show. She has also written articles for several of the major magazines for women.

Name _____

For Thinking and Discussing

1. As a child she was a tomboy and her height of six feet made her want to become a basketball star. What changed her goal to that of becoming a novelist?

_____
_____
_____
_____

2. Who were the main influences on Julia Child in her career in French cooking?

_____
_____
_____
_____

3. What was the occasion of the transition between Julia Child's career as a writer and that of a television personality?

_____
_____
_____
_____

4. What is Julia Child's basic philosophy on the art of good French cooking?

_____
_____
_____
_____

Name _____

5. How did her personality and method of presentation add to the popularity and credibility of her TV show *The French Chef*?

_____
_____
_____
_____
_____
_____
_____
_____

For Further Research

Find out how French cooking differs from the American preparation of food. What are the French techniques? Describe how a typically "American" dish could be prepared the French way and how the end results would be different.

SHIRLEY CHISHOLM

Shirley Chisholm marks her own place in American history by being the first black woman to serve in Congress. From the very beginning of her first term, she became an outspoken chairperson of bills to revise Social Security laws, criticize military spending and encourage equality between races, ethnic groups and men and women. She was often regarded as a "thorn" in the side of some of her fellow Congressmen, but she always had the courage to stand up for what she wanted.

She was born in 1924 in Brooklyn's impoverished Bedford-Stuyvesant section to a father who was an emigrant from Guyana and a mother who had been a native of Barbados. When she was three years old, she was sent to Barbados to live for a while with her grandmother on a farm. During those early years her grandmother taught her the virtues of pride, courage and faith, and she was very stern in her efforts with Shirley. She returned to Brooklyn at the age of eleven, having acquired a British elementary school education and a West Indies rhythm of speech that remains. After graduating from a girls' high school in Brooklyn she enrolled in Brooklyn College. It was there in college when the roots of politics were implanted in her mind. After earning an M.A. in education at Columbia University, she became director of Friends Day Nursery and later became recognized as an authority on early childhood education. While a member of the teaching profession, she was quietly establishing credibility among black voters within the Democratic Party machine. Her election victory in 1954 to the New York Assembly got her off to the right start in politics and she won again in 1965 and 1966. In 1968 the bounds of her congressional district were redrawn, and she decided to run for Congress in a district that was about 70% black or Puerto Rican. The odds worked to her advantage and she was elected. Once she got there, she made it well-known that she would not be taking a backseat in Congress. Time and time again she also crossed party lines on several occasions and became something of a maverick within the Democratic Party. In 1972 she launched a campaign for the presidential election and although she lost, her name became well-established in American homes. In 1982 she decided to leave Congress, citing administrations that were unresponsive and a feeling of hopelessness that could not make her effective.

Name _____

For Thinking and Discussing

1. How did it happen that Mrs. Emmeline Seale, Shirley Chisholm's grandmother, had such a lasting impact on Shirley's life?

_____

_____

_____

_____

2. How did Shirley Chisholm become involved in politics, when she had trained to be an elementary education teacher?

_____

_____

_____

_____

3. Why was Shirley Chisholm less than satisfactory to the Democratic Party machine even though she had them convinced she could win a large share of the black vote and would be a popular candidate?

_____

_____

_____

_____

4. It has been said that Shirley Chisholm is in a sense a lot like Susan B. Anthony. What reason(s) can you cite for this parallel?

_____

_____

_____

_____

Name _____

5. Why did Shirley Chisholm decide in 1982 to leave politics?

_____

_____

_____

_____

_____

_____

_____

_____

For Further Research

During her years in Congress, Shirley Chisholm has not only been outspoken; she has also taken great strides toward social change. Discuss some of the issues she faced and how she handled them.

AMELIA EARHART

Amelia Earhart was the first woman to fly across the Atlantic and also the first to solo it alone. She was the first flyer to solo between Hawaii and the American mainland. In 1937 she attempted to fly completely around the world. On the longest over-water leg, from New Guinea to Howland Island, her plane disappeared without a trace. With her when the plane vanished was her navigator Fred Noonan. The result was one of the most intriguing search stories ever. Amelia Earhart's brief flying career had lasted only nine years but her many accomplishments, including being the first woman ever awarded the Distinguished Flying Cross, stand as an inspiration to other women. Her career as an aviatrix began shortly after she dropped out of Columbia University to earn money for flying lessons. She always encouraged women to fly and became the aviation editor of *Cosmopolitan* as well as being one of the founders of Ninety-Nines, an international organization of women pilots. The mystery surrounding her strange disappearance has become almost as well remembered as her accomplishments.

In 1966 Fred Goerner, a newsman for station KCBS in San Francisco, became extremely interested in the Earhart case and launched into a most intensive search for the truth about her disappearance. Her story began as a result of an interview with a former Japanese named Josephine Akiyama, who claimed to have been an eye witness to Amelia's capture by the Japanese on the island of Saipan in 1937. His remarkable story, called *The Search for Amelia Earhart,* spanned six long years of research and included four expeditions to the Western Pacific Marianas and Marshall islands. Goerner interviewed everyone he could find who was even remotely connected with the case, and he spent hours and hours pouring over government files and the testimony of State Department witnesses. His conclusion was that Amelia Earhart and her navigator, Fred Noonan, had diverted their main course of announced travel to investigate unofficially Japanese warfields to Truk in the Central Caroline Chain of Islands. He theorized that they probably encountered bad weather and fuel shortage problems. They then force landed the plane on an island owned by the Japanese, were captured, and later executed. While his story is based on his extensive research, other theories of her demise still exist.

Name _____

For Thinking and Discussing

1. What message did Amelia Earhart have for women interested in flying?

   _____

   _____

   _____

   _____

2. How are accomplishments like those of Amelia Earhart important to a society such as ours?

   _____

   _____

   _____

   _____

   _____

3. What was Amelia Earhart's goal when she was last seen?

   _____

   _____

   _____

   _____

4. If Goerner's conclusion is correct about what really happened to Amelia Earhart, how does this change her place in history?

   _____

   _____

   _____

   _____

Name _____

5. Why do you think the U.S. government would have been reluctant to acknowledge the "mission" Goerner alleges she was on?

_____

_____

_____

_____

_____

_____

_____

_____

For Further Research

Fred Goerner's book *The Search for Amelia Earhart* makes for some very interesting reading about her disappearance. Read this book and find out the full explanation for his conclusion.

CHRIS EVERT

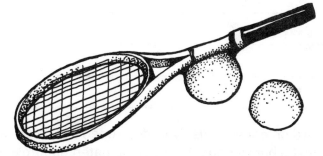

Chris Evert began winning tennis tournaments when she was only eight years old, and by the time she was twenty, she was ranked as America's best female player. Her record of championships and money won would alone place her in history among the best ever, but the graceful way she handled her success and her religious background have made her an inspiration and role model for other young women to follow.

She was born in 1954 in Fort Lauderdale, Florida, the daughter of a father who was a professional tennis teacher and former champion. Chris' two brothers and two sisters also played tennis, so it was the natural thing for her to do at a very young age. Chris fell in love with the game when she was only six years old, and she spent many, many hours after school and on weekends practicing her game. The practice paid off as she developed over those early years a style all her own that consisted of a strong, two-handed backhand stroke that dominates her game. Chris also learned patience and poise and outlasted many of her opponents by simply routinely going on with her game until they made the mistakes.

She began to make a name for herself in 1970 when she beat Margaret Smith Court. Chris shortly thereafter was named to the Wightman Cup Team, being the youngest player (at 16) to compete with the British. Her stunning victory over Virginia Wade gave the United States the Cup and won her the Most Valuable Player award. Many matches with Billie Jean King followed with "Chrissy" winning her share. She was successful both on and off the court and was idolized by thousands of devoted fans. Chris Evert became the first player in women's tennis to win a million dollars, and her winning the U.S. Open six times has been accomplished by two others. She has also been recognized as one of the finest ever (if not the best) female tennis players on a clay surface.

But her place in history goes beyond the tennis court. Her attractive face and figure made her a hit with men, and her youth made her the idol of teenagers everywhere. Her values and moral code brought her loyalty and following among middle-aged mothers. In short she was "Miss America Pie." She was at one time engaged to tennis champion Jimmy Connors, but the couple split up because of their careers and she later married John Lloyd.

Name _____

For Thinking and Discussing

1. How did Chris Evert's environment help make her learning the game of tennis at a very young age the "natural" thing to do?

   _____

   _____

   _____

   _____

2. In those early years of long hours of hard practice, Chris Evert developed a style of game that was all her own and would later make her famous. What is the patented stroke she perfected that dominates her game and why is it so successful?

   _____

   _____

   _____

   _____

3. Although she had won several junior tournaments, the name of Chris Evert really began to surface as a star when, at the age of 16, she defeated Margaret Smith Court in a tournament shortly after Court had just made history by winning the Grand Slam of Women's Tennis. What tournaments are included in this cluster of prestigious tournaments?

   _____

   _____

   _____

4. The record of Chris Evert stands today as one of the finest ever. But her popularity as a sports idol went beyond the tennis court. Aside from her game, what made her the idol of thousands?

   _____

   _____

   _____

Name _____

5. Chris Evert was at one time engaged to male tennis star Jimmy Connors. Their romance seemed a natural to America. What caused this celebrated pair to break off their engagement?

_____

_____

_____

_____

_____

_____

_____

For Further Research

The career of Chris Evert has been highlighted by many tennis championships and also personal achievements that honored her talents and personality. Cite those achievements in her career she cherishes the most.

GERALDINE FERRARO

The 1984 presidential election held a special historical significance as Geraldine Ferraro was chosen as the running mate of Democratic candidate Walter Mondale, thus becoming the first woman to be nominated by a major party for that office. Even though the Mondale-Ferraro ticket was defeated in the election, women everywhere proclaimed her running for such an office a victory for the advancement for women's equality.

Ferraro was born in 1935 in Newburgh, New York, the daughter of a restaurant owner. After Ferraro's father's death, her mother moved the family to less expensive housing. Geraldine graduated from Marymount College, then entered Fordham University Law School. She met John Zaccaro, a Manhattan real estate developer and married him, but she chose to keep her maiden name out of devotion to her mother. The couple then had three children, and Ferraro delayed her career for fourteen years to raise them.

In 1974 she became an assistant district attorney for the Special Victims Bureau. Her clients were victims of rape and child abuse, and she developed a reputation as a tough prosecuter who showed no mercy. Frustration at her job and dissatisfaction with her boss led her away from the D.A.'s office into politics. She favored the working class and chose a tough district in Queens for her first political battle, which she won. Ferraro took her new position seriously and soon became adept at gaining what she wanted for the people she represented. Ferraro earned high marks for her voting record within the Democratic Party though she crossed party lines on the issues of busing, military preparedness, and the nuclear arms defense. Her appointment as 1984 Democratic Platform Committee chairperson was the break that propelled her into the limelight. Capitalizing on an abundant exposure to the media, she gained approval of the party for the thematic approach she took while building the party platform. Pressure from women's groups scorned by the defeat of ERA caused Mondale, the party's choice, to consider choosing a woman as his running mate. Even though few thought he would really choose a woman, he shocked the world by announcing Ferraro as his choice. She was not only a well-qualified person, but also politically appealing in that she could help draw Italian-American votes and hopefully much of the Catholic vote.

Name _____

For Thinking and Discussing

1. Why did Geraldine Ferraro remain Ferraro even after she married real estate developer John Zaccaro?

_____

_____

_____

_____

2. How did Ferraro develop a reputation as a tough assistant district attorney who showed no mercy when it came to dealing with those who had victimized her clients?

_____

_____

_____

_____

3. How did Geraldine Ferraro lose favor in her party by her voting record on busing, military spending and the nuclear arms race?

_____

_____

_____

_____

4. Why did Walter Mondale find Ferraro politically appealing when he chose her for his running mate in 1984?

_____

_____

_____

_____

Name _____

5. It was said that Ferraro was able to get along with her male colleagues in Congress better than fellow women predecessors like Shirley Chisholm and Bella Abzug. How was she able to do this and maintain her effectiveness as a legislator?

_____

_____

_____

_____

_____

_____

_____

For Further Research

Even though Geraldine Ferraro was politically appealing to Walter Mondale, who certainly had good reasons for choosing her as his running mate in 1984, they lost the election by a wide margin. Check the records and the explanations of that race and find out the reasons political analysts say they were defeated.

JANE FONDA

Jane Fonda is one of the best known women in America as she has reached the public eye on three fronts: the theater and motion pictures, social reform, and her published books on fitness and exercise. Her achievements and awards as an actress stand above her other talents, but her activism during the war in Vietnam and her advice on staying trim have all combined to make Jane Fonda a household name.

She was born in 1937 in New York City, the daughter of famous actor Henry Fonda and Frances Seymour Brokaw, a widow with family ties dating back to English royalty. Although her father never tried to influence Jane into an acting career as a child, he recognized her talent and hoped she would somehow, someday make that decision. Her mother suffered a mental illness and died when Jane was thirteen. Despite the economic advantages created by her father's success on the stage and in films, Jane and her brother Peter did not have a very happy childhood. Their happiest times were spent at their New England-style farmhouse on Tigertail Road in the hills above Hollywood, California.

After secondary school, Jane enrolled in fashionable Vassar College to study art and ballet. After her first year her aunt convinced her to appear with her father in *The Country Girl* in Omaha, Nebraska, and the next summer she appeared in *The Male Animal* on Cape Cod. She then went to Paris to study art, but returned in the summer of 1958, still unsure of what she wanted to do. Then she met Lee Strasberg, a well-known acting teacher and he accepted Jane as a private student. It was Lee Strasberg who made her the accomplished actress she is today. Once he convinced her "The Method" (his method wherein actors learned to experience rather than imitate the roles they played) was the way to master acting, she became a devout student and she spent many long hours perfecting her talent. One successful film followed another and led to an eventual Oscar as best actress for the 1971 thriller *Klute.* After that she began to choose films that conveyed the social messages for which she stood. Her stands against the war in Vietnam, against the use of nuclear energy and for equal rights for women have made Jane Fonda a controversial star.

Name _____

For Thinking and Discussing

1. Even though her father did not try to influence her as a child toward a career in acting, explain why his own career no doubt had a bearing on Jane Fonda becoming a stage and screen star.

   _____

   _____

   _____

   _____

2. Jane Fonda's success as an accomplished actress is due at least in part to the training she received from veteran teacher Lee Strasberg, who taught acting through what he called ''The Method.'' Explain his philosophy on acting.

   _____

   _____

   _____

   _____

3. More recently, Jane Fonda's image in the eye of the public has shifted to a new role as a physical fitness expert. What advice does she have for the women of America and how has she gone about creating her popular new image?

   _____

   _____

   _____

   _____

4. Why does Jane Fonda choose roles in movies that are controversial and provocative?

   _____

   _____

   _____

   _____

Name _____

5. Jane Fonda once played the role of Norma Brown in a play called *Invitation to a March* in which she received this advice from an older woman: "What I did, I did because it was right for me. There's a little bell inside that tells you what's right for you. When it rings, you open the door and go!" How does this advice relate to the life of Jane Fonda?

_____

_____

_____

_____

_____

_____

_____

For Further Research

Jane Fonda is best known as a star of the stage and screen. However, she is also widely known for her activism during the 1970's. Research the issues she took and the stands she took that made her such a subject of controversy.

KATHARINE HEPBURN

SHOWING NOW:
"The African Queen"

Perhaps Katharine Hepburn ranks as *the* first lady of the American cinema. Her career spans five decades, and she will always be remembered as a remarkably versatile actress who did equally well in a wide variety of roles. She was born into an upper-class Scots-Yankee family in 1909 in Hartford, Connecticut. Her father was a urologist and her mother was active in the suffrage movement. She learned self-discipline early, beginning each day with a cold shower. As a child she was a tomboy and she received her formal education at home through tutors, at the Hartford School for Girls and at Bryn Mawr College. She wanted to become a physician, but she gave that idea up because there were so few women in medicine. She next set her sights on becoming an actress, and after receiving her B.A. in 1928, she went immediately into summer stock theater. In 1932 she got her first big break playing the role of Antiope in *The Warrior's Husband.* She signed an exclusive contract with RKO Pictures and received her first nomination for best actress for her portrayal of the stagestruck tomboy in *Morning Glory.* There followed a series of several box office successes in the next few years. However, she was not popular at RKO because she refused to accept roles she did not like. By 1937 the friction was intolerable and she bought out her contract and began working for Columbia Pictures.

She returned to Broadway with the highly successful *Philadelphia Story,* a play written specifically for her. In 1942 she began her long association, both professionally and personally, with Spencer Tracy in *Woman of the Year.* Her subsequent MGM films with Tracy were all box office successes. Her career seemed on an endless streak until she reached its nadir with *The Iron Petticoats.* She bounced back quickly and won her fifth Academy Award nomination as the prim and proper lady missionary opposite Humphrey Bogart, who played a rough alcoholic riverboat captain in *The African Queen.*

In the early 1960's she stopped making movies to care for her ailing friend Spencer Tracy. In 1967 she came back with her second best actress nomination with *Guess Who's Coming to Dinner,* opposite Tracy. Her dear friend passed away shortly after the film's release. She busied herself and passed her sorrow by doing several films in quick succession culminating with her award-winning performance opposite Henry Fonda in *On Golden Pond.*

Name _____

For Thinking and Discussing

1. How did Katharine Hepburn's early childhood prepare her for the discipline she would need for a career in acting?

   _____

   _____

   _____

   _____

2. How did her education prepare her for her career as a film and stage star?

   _____

   _____

   _____

   _____

3. How did Katharine Hepburn's film career begin?

   _____

   _____

   _____

   _____

   _____

4. How would Katharine Hepburn describe a typical Hepburn-Tracy film?

   _____

   _____

   _____

   _____

Name _____

5. Katharine Hepburn once said when asked what she thought about the refusal of many young people to accept responsibility, ''You really have to make a choice. You can't survive without character for long.'' What did she mean by this statement?

_____

_____

_____

_____

_____

_____

_____

For Further Research

Katharine Hepburn's long and successful film career has been accented by a number of distinguished awards and nominations. Research her nominations by the Academy of Motion Picture Arts and Sciences including the four pictures for which she received best actress nominations as well as other noteworthy nominations she has received.

MAHALIA JACKSON

The joys and sorrows, the tragedies and triumphs of life itself were all expressed in the music of Mahalia Jackson, one of the greatest gospel singers of all time. Her voice combined a powerful vitality with a deep religious conviction. Although her singing style revealed the strong influence of the city's musical flavor, she preferred to be identified with religious music. She decided in the 1930's to devote her life to spreading the word of God and embarked on a singing career.

Mahalia Jackson was born in the city of music—New Orleans, Louisiana—in 1911 on Water Street between the railroad track and the levee of the Mississippi. Her family was very religious, and she grew up in an environment filled with gospel and spiritual music. She often daydreamed about moving to the North where there was less prejudice and Blacks could have a chance at a better life. When she was sixteen, she finally made the move to Chicago where she worked as a hotel maid and packed dates in a food plant. The church remained at the core of her life, and she was quite happy with her life in the predominantly black South Side of Chicago. The Great Depression brought an end to that good life, and she began singing with a gospel group making about $1.50 a night. Once she made her commitment to sing for the Lord, she literally poured her entire soul into her singing, and her style was criticized by high-society Blacks. In 1938 she met and later married Isaac Hockenhull, who wanted her to become a blues singer. The couple eventually divorced when Ike constantly criticized her devotion to gospel singing and she his gambling at the racetrack.

By the end of the Depression gospel music had reached a new high in popularity, and she got her first break recording the song "I Will Move on Up a Little Higher." It became known as her song and *Movin' on Up* was the title of her biography. From there her career mushroomed into full bloom. She appeared in the top concert halls all over the United States, but she refused to appear in nightclubs, saying she only sang two kinds of songs, one for Blacks who liked to tap their feet and one for those who liked religious songs sung to them. In 1960 she was honored by President Kennedy to sing "The Star-Spangled Banner" at his inauguration. Her tour of Europe thrilled thousands of fans, even though many could not understand the words of her songs. Mahalia Jackson died in 1972—to be remembered as one of the greatest gospel singers of all time, a lady who never compromised her principles.

Name _____

For Thinking and Discussing

1. How was the city in which Mahalia Jackson was born reflected in her music?

   _____

   _____

   _____

   _____

2. As a child, Mahalia Jackson heard many stories about the "land to the North," and she longed to go there herself. Why did she move to Chicago?

   _____

   _____

   _____

   _____

3. As a singer during the Depression with the Johnston Gospel Singers, Mahalia Jackson decided to take a professional singing lesson from Professor DuBois, a black tenor who owned a music salon in Chicago. Why was the lesson her one and only?

   _____

   _____

   _____

   _____

4. Describe the unhappy marriage of Mahalia Jackson and Isaac Hockenhull and how it came to an end.

   _____

   _____

   _____

   _____

Name _____

5. Why did Mahalia Jackson refuse nightclub appearances which could have made her a lot of money and why did she want to sing only gospel and religious music?

_____

_____

_____

_____

_____

_____

_____

_____

For Further Research

Through her years of travel and exposure in the public eye, Mahalia Jackson developed some very strong feelings about the evils of racial prejudice and about interracial marriage. Research those feelings and discuss why you think she felt that way.

LADY BIRD JOHNSON

The quiet simple wedding ceremony on November 17, 1934, in St. Mark's historic Episcopalian Church in San Antonio, Texas, was held without fanfare and without the slightest hint of the politically powerful union that had just taken place. The young Southern belle had resisted the hazards of a hasty marriage (the courtship lasted less than two months), even though her father insisted that "some of the best deals are made in a hurry." But when Lyndon Johnson won over the heart of her father to his side, she went against the wishes of her Aunt Effie, who had helped to raise her, and she said yes to the lanky Texan. She would later borrow ten thousand dollars against her inheritance to help finance his first campaign for Congress, a position that would ultimately lead to his becoming President of the United States and she becoming its First Lady.

She was born Claudia Alta Taylor in Karnack, Texas, in 1912. Her black nursemaid said once when she was only two years old that she was "as purty as a Lady Bird." So did her father and the name stuck with her. Her mother was the daughter of a wealthy Alabama aristocrat, and her father, a man of Spanish descent, was a farmer. When Lady Bird was five, her mother, who was pregnant, fell down a flight of stairs and died. Her mother's unmarried sister, Aunt Effie, came to live with the family and exerted a great influence on Lady Bird during her formative years.

After graduating from high school in Alabama, Lady Bird enrolled at St. Mary's School for Girls in Austin, Texas, and she immediately fell in love with the city. Her graduation present from her father was a trip to Washington, D.C. It was there she met the congressional secretary Lyndon Baines Johnson, who would soon become her husband. When a congressman died from Johnson's home district, a special election was held and Johnson won the election. When Johnson became Vice President, Jacqueline Kennedy called on Lady Bird to undertake many of the receptions and political trips that had previously fallen on the First Lady. When her husband became President after the tragic death of John F. Kennedy, Lady Bird became the nation's First Lady, a role she filled with grace and charm. When LBJ was elected in his own right, she knew exactly what she wanted to do. Her Beautification of America and the work she did for her husband's War on Poverty and Head Start programs rank her as one of the top humanitarians among our First Ladies.

Name _____

For Thinking and Discussing

1. How did Claudia Alta Taylor acquire the nickname "Lady Bird"?

   _____
   _____
   _____
   _____

2. What did Lady Bird's father mean by the statement: "Some of the best deals are made in a hurry"?

   _____
   _____
   _____
   _____

3. How did Lady Bird help her husband in his political campaign, first in his bid for Congress, then again in 1964 when he ran for President in his own right?

   _____
   _____
   _____
   _____

4. Why would Lady Bird be called a good businesswoman?

   _____
   _____
   _____
   _____

Name _____

5. Lady Bird once said: "The great effort of women is not, I believe, to invade a man's world. . . but to be a full partner in a warm compassionate world." What would she have to say about the feminist equal rights movement among women?

_____

_____

_____

_____

_____

_____

_____

_____

For Further Research

Lady Bird's place in history is marked by her humanitarian and conservation program she initiated as First Lady. Find out the nature of her efforts and cite some of the things she accomplished.

HELEN KELLER

Helen Keller was stricken with a rare brain disease before she was two years of age, and her world suddenly went without sight and sound. She could no longer communicate with others and faced an unknown world of silence and darkness for the rest of her life. Shortly before Helen was seven, her father took her to Dr. Alexander Graham Bell, who suggested they contact the Perkins Institute for the Blind in Boston, Massachusetts.

Anne Sullivan from Boston was then hired to become Helen's teacher. Anne had been nearly blind herself as a child but had her sight restored by surgery. Early communication was established with Helen by touching and spelling words on her hand. When she was able to associate objects in the real world with words, progress began to occur rapidly. She worked out an alphabet and within a short time had converted Helen to Braille. By the time she was ten years old, she had learned to speak. She loved nature and all its glory, especially animals. When she was a little girl, Anne took her to the zoo and Helen was able to touch some of the trained animals. Her experience was unforgettable.

Helen enrolled at Radcliffe College and graduated with honors in 1904. She spent the rest of her life giving lectures, writing books, and making public appearances in the hope of encouraging and assisting those who were blind through her own personal example of a living inspiration.

After World War II, she visited wounded veterans in hospitals all over the world. She spoke in England, France, Italy, and Greece on behalf of the physically handicapped. In 1964 she was awarded the Presidential Medal of Freedom. Her books include *The Story of My Life, Midstream—My Later Life, Let Us Have Faith, Out of the Dark* and *The Open Door.* Her life story became the subject of a successful play called *The Miracle Worker.* Helen Keller died in 1968.

Name _____

For Thinking and Discussing

1. Because she was blind and deaf, Helen Keller developed her remaining senses far beyond their normal capabilities. Of those remaining (taste, touch, and smell), which do you think would be most useful, and how would you go about making it stronger to help you better cope with the world?

_____
_____
_____
_____

2. Which of the senses is most important to you and why would it be so difficult for you to give up?

_____
_____
_____
_____

3. Close your eyes and plug up your ears and remain that way for several moments. What were the thoughts that were going through your mind during this period of time?

_____
_____
_____
_____

4. To a blind person, would it be better to have been born that way and never experienced the joy of sight, or would it be better to have been born with sight (experience sight for, say five years) and then lose it? Defend your choice.

_____
_____
_____
_____

Name _____

5. Take your choice from among the following and provide a vivid, lifelike description to someone who has been denied the experience of that which you are describing. Be certain to use words and terms that will overemphasize your description to the handicapped.

    The glory and majesty of a morning sunrise (or evening sunset)
    The beautiful sounds of a famous symphony orchestra
    The taste of a banana split
    The smell of the world itself following a fresh spring rain
    The touch of a baby's skin

_____

_____

_____

_____

For Further Research

Find out about how blind people can get Seeing Eye dogs, as well as other benefits that are available to them to make their lives richer and more meaningful.

CORETTA KING

Because of her dedication to the peace movement started by her late husband, Coretta King has come to be regarded as an effective and powerful figure in her own right within the movement. During the dark days following her husband's assassination in 1968, her quiet dignity and control paralleled that of Jacqueline Kennedy a few years earlier. Her work since his death has become a symbol of all that Dr. Martin Luther King, Jr., stood for.

She was born in 1927 in Heiberger, Alabama, of parents who owned "family land" handed down through the generations since the Civil War, but her parents were not wealthy. As a child Coretta was forced to walk five miles to school each day in Heiberger. Each day the school bus carrying white children passed her by, and she was determined to someday fight for equality. She went to Lincoln School, a private missionary institution in Marion, and there became convinced that education was the key to a better life. At Antioch College she gained a teaching degree but decided by graduation to pursue a career in voice and piano.

It was in Boston at the New England Conservatory of Music that she met the young Atlanta minister working on his doctorate who would become her husband. Realizing that their goals were similar, she gave up her pursuit of a career in music and the couple was married. Dr. King became minister of a Baptist Church in Montgomery, Alabama. A short time later he became involved in the civil rights crusade when he became interested in the bus boycotting issue. It soon became apparent their lives would not be like that of an ordinary family, and Coretta became more actively involved. She went where her husband went, and she performed several "freedom concerts," displaying her musical talents in portraying the civil rights movement. Violence threatened her family on more than one occasion, but her answer when asked how she and Dr. King could jeopardize their family was simply, "We have faith in God and try to be good parents." Her faith was tested when Dr. King was assassinated on April 4, 1968, while he was in Memphis demonstrating for the striking garbage collectors. The aftermath of his death left her with the responsibility to carry on with the work he had started. Her place in history will perhaps be best remembered for the dignity and courage and effectiveness of her appearances following his death.

Name _____

For Thinking and Discussing

1. What convinced Coretta King as a child of the need to fight for equality among races?

   _____

   _____

   _____

   _____

2. When she was in secondary school in Marion, Alabama, she concluded that education was the only way for her to escape the restrictions and prejudice of her environment, so she went to college, got a degree, then pursued a career in music at the New England Conservatory of Music. What caused her to abandon her goal of a career in music?

   _____

   _____

   _____

   _____

3. How was Coretta King's life as a mother raising four children to change when her husband became actively involved in the civil rights movement?

   _____

   _____

   _____

   _____

4. How was the behavior of Coretta King similar to that of Jacqueline Kennedy during the time following the assassinations of their husbands?

   _____

   _____

   _____

   _____

Name _____

5. How did she react to James Earl Ray, the man who was captured and convicted of her husband's assassination and sentenced to ninety-nine years in prison?

_____

_____

_____

_____

_____

_____

_____

For Further Research

Since the assassination of her husband in 1968, Coretta King has become actively involved in several of his earlier efforts. Research and cite examples of some of the efforts and achievements she has made since his death.

CLARA BOOTHE LUCE

Clara Boothe Luce became famous as an author and successful playwright. Later she was elected to Congress in 1942 and then served as the United States Ambassador to Italy from 1953 to 1957. Although her success was not generally applauded by other women, she nevertheless has made her mark in history through her accomplishments and tough, rugged honesty. Her most successful play *The Women* no doubt had something to do with her less than popular status among women, as the only nice female in her play is the least interesting. She also wrote *Kiss the Boys Goodbye* and *Margin for Error.* Although controversy seemed to follow her wherever she went, it was her own integrity she felt most important and thus she stood up for what she believed, even when her choices were sometimes unpopular and caused her to be the object of criticism.

She was twenty years old when she married George Brokaw, a wealthy New Yorker who was several years her senior. The marriage ended in divorce and she set out on a career as a writer and editor. She became an editor of *Vogue* and managing editor of *Vanity Fair* before she married Henry Luce, the famous publisher of *Time, Life,* and *Fortune* magazines.

From that point she launched her career in politics. In 1940 she campaigned for Wendell Wilkie, the Republican candidate for President. Her effective public speaking ability brought her the honor of giving a keynote speech at the 1944 Republican National Convention. The death of her teenage daughter in an automobile accident led to her retirement from Congress in 1947. She then became a Roman Catholic and began writing on religious subjects. In 1952 she got back into politics vigorously supporting Republican Dwight D. Eisenhower. When he won the election, Eisenhower appointed her as U.S. Ambassador to Italy. She became the second woman to receive the rank of ambassador and the first to be assigned to an important country like Italy. She served in the position between 1953 and 1957. Once again her caustic sense of humor caused her to be the center of controversy. In 1959 Eisenhower again appointed her Ambassador, this time to Brazil. After a bitter debate in the U.S. Senate over her approval, she was finally given the necessary Senate okay. Because of the quarrel that had erupted, Mrs. Luce resigned from the position a few days later feeling that it would be in the best interests of the position. She did continue to serve on several boards and commissions.

Name _____

For Thinking and Discussing

1. What brought Clara Boothe Luce's career in politics to national attention and much publicity with her support of Wendell Wilkie?

   _____

   _____

   _____

   _____

2. How did her popular play *The Women* make her less than popular among women?

   _____

   _____

   _____

   _____

3. What was there about the personality of Clara Boothe Luce that made her often the center of controversy?

   _____

   _____

   _____

   _____

4. Because she was an excellent public speaker and because she was devoted to the Republican Party, she was asked to present a woman's point of view at the 1944 National Republican Convention. She said she would decline the offer unless she could present her speech during an evening session when the press and radio would be there. Why do you think she made such a demand? (Incidentally, she was granted her wish.)

   _____

   _____

   _____

Name _____

5. Why did she resign her assignment as U.S. Ambassador to Brazil before she ever assumed the post?

_____

_____

_____

_____

_____

_____

_____

_____

For Further Research

Research the beginning of Clara Boothe Luce's career in politics, including her interest in the New Nationalist Party.

DOLLEY MADISON

Perhaps she is remembered best as the First Lady who brought elegance and fashion and tradition to the new nation. She had a style all her own that made her legendary in Washington society, but she was also well-remembered for her charm and her kindness. Her role as a master diplomat saved the day on many occasions for her husband from his political enemies.

She was born in Guilford County, North Carolina, the daughter of John Payne, a Virginia Quaker, who raised his daughter in the strictest of traditions. She married John Todd, a Quaker lawyer, but he died of yellow fever leaving her a widow at an early age. She was admired by many, but one of her suitors, Senator Aaron Burr, introduced her to James Madison, a 43-year-old confirmed bachelor, who was a member of the House of Representatives. Dolley represented everything he had waited for and their romance swept Philadelphia.

The Madison homestead called Montpelier, was located near Monticello, the estate of Thomas Jefferson, and the two men became best friends. When Jefferson became President, he appointed Madison Secretary of State, and Dolley was once again thrust into the limelight in Washington. Because of her excellent taste, Jefferson also called on Dolley to serve as his official hostess on most occasions. This plus the entertaining she did for her husband soon earned her the reputation of a social leader in Washington. When her husband became President, her role of First Lady placed her in an even stronger role to dominate Washington society. She cultivated the right friendship with the right people, often helping to overcome problems created by political enemies of her husband. When the British marched on Washington during the War of 1812, Dolley risked her life removing the state treasures just before they set fire to the Palace. Following the War, the Madisons returned to Montpelier. There Dolley helped her husband turn his years of copious notes into a manuscript. Madison's failing health caused her to end up doing much of the work, and when he died, she finished the manuscript herself. She was able to sell the first half, but the money didn't last and she was forced to sell all of Montpelier except the family cemetery. Penniless, she remained well-respected in Washington society, being supported by those she had served so well. Congress finally authorized the purchase of the remaining Madison papers, and Dolley had at least some money to live out the rest of her life till she died in 1849.

Name _____

For Thinking and Discussing

1. Describe the courtship of Dolley Todd and the 43-year-old bachelor James Madison.

   _____
   _____
   _____
   _____

2. Why was Dolley's style in entertaining guests so immensely popular in Washington society?

   _____
   _____
   _____
   _____

3. How did Dolley Madison help to complement her husband's role as President of the United States?

   _____
   _____
   _____
   _____

4. Dolley Madison is well-remembered as the First Lady who brought elegance and fashion to the presidency. Why is she remembered for this?

   _____
   _____
   _____
   _____

Name _____

5. Although she would have denied the role, Dolley Madison was known as a master politi-
    cian without ever realizing it. Why do historians credit her with this stereotype?

    _____

    _____

    _____

    _____

    _____

    _____

    _____

    _____

For Further Research

Although they served as First Lady in different eras, there are certain similarities in taste and
style between Dolley Madison and Jacqueline Kennedy Onassis. Point out some of these
similarities.

MARGARET MEAD

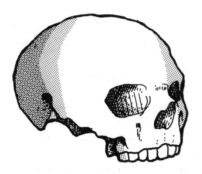

Margaret Mead earned her place in American history by becoming one of its foremost anthropologists. Her studies of how culture influences the development of personality were widely read and contributed a great deal to the growing plethora of anthropological knowledge. She lived among the people of Samoa and other South Sea islands for many years, and her findings describe how cultures differ in the behaviors they consider appropriate.

Margaret Mead was born in Philadelphia and spent her school days in Pennsylvania schools. She then spent a year at DePauw University before transferring to Barnard College in New York, where she graduated. It was there that she fell under the influence of anthropologists Ruth Benedict and Franz Boas, who would encourage and inspire her to a lifelong career in anthropology. Mead was also, no doubt, influenced in her youth by her mother, a sociologist who studied Italian immigrants. Her travels to the South Sea as a very young woman alone among primitive people broke all the rules of conventional society and were shocking to many. Her reason for becoming so involved in the study of cultures was to help Americans better understand themselves. Without the power of the written word nor the ability to record its history, those primitive cultures she observed had only word of mouth to pass their culture on to the next generation. Mead felt that this kind of "passing on" from one generation to the next can and should be built into our own lives as well. The family as a unit would be much closer if we were perhaps more dependent upon our parents and grandparents for learning what we know. But she also felt that even though understanding other generations and cultures would help to bridge the gap, nonetheless each person is a product of his own generation only, and the secret lies in learning to understand and accept the ways of the generation and other cultures.

During her later years, Mead devoted a lot of her time to writing and speaking and serving in various capacities on committees, commissions and boards associated with science and human welfare. She was also very active in the National Institute of Mental Health and the World Federation for Mental Health. She became Curator Emeritus of Ethnology at the American Museum of Natural History in 1970. She died in 1978, leaving behind a legacy of her years of research and the findings she made.

Name _____

For Thinking and Discussing

1. What people can you name who were influences on Margaret Mead's choosing a career in anthropology?

   _____
   _____
   _____
   _____

2. What was Margaret Mead's main reason for devoting her life to the study of other cultures?

   _____
   _____
   _____
   _____

3. Even though she believed very strongly in studying cultures to help bridge the gap between generations, Margaret Mead insisted that each generation was different from all others and should be recognized as such. Explain what she meant by this statement.

   _____
   _____
   _____
   _____

4. In her autobiography *Blackberry Winter,* Margaret Mead suggests that the world of anthropology is wide open to those who are willing to take a chance. With the vast body of knowledge about cultures already recorded, what horizons remain open to anthropologists?

   _____
   _____
   _____
   _____

Name _____

5. How did Margaret Mead spend her later years serving her profession and earning her niche in history?

_____

_____

_____

_____

_____

_____

_____

_____

For Further Research

Read Margaret Mead's best-seller *Coming of Age in Samoa.* Then compare and contrast the life-styles of these primitive people with that of our own society today.

GRANDMA MOSES

Her name was Anna Mary Robertson Moses. She was better known to America as Grandma Moses. Her success story is unique in the fact that she sold her first painting when she was seventy-eight years old! At the age of eighty she became an overwhelming success and her paintings became very popular.

She was born in the green meadows of Washington County, New York, in 1860, of Scotch-Irish ancestry. She was one of a family of ten children and she spent her first twelve years there. Her first experience at painting came when her father brought home some white paper. She drew her pictures first, then colored them with grape juice and berries. When she was sixteen, she began working for Mr. and Mrs. Sylvester James. There Anna Robertson met the hired hand Thomas Moses and married him in 1887. The couple accepted a job in North Carolina managing a horse ranch; however, on their trip south they got no further than the Shenandoah Valley of Virginia. There they took over the ownership of a hundred-acre farm.

Anna, like her mother had before her, bore ten children of her own. However, one only lived six weeks and four others were stillborn, so only five grew to adulthood. The family then migrated back north to a home near where Anna had lived as a child.

Anna had always enjoyed painting but had usually painted only little pictures for Christmas gifts, and she was never serious about her painting. After Thomas passed away, she began painting more frequently, and one day an art collector from New York City passed through town and bought all her paintings. He took them to the city and displayed them in galleries, and her scenes of the rural world in which she had lived for so many years became in great demand. She had enjoyed painting when she had the time, which, because of her years of hard farm labor and raising children, had been very seldom. But she had the time in her later years and she painted often, much to the joy of those who liked her work. The popularity of her work seemed to offer something for everyone. Her straight forward images that reaffirmed the values of America's rural heritage and her colorful folk paintings were hung in museum's and art galleries all over the world. Grandma Moses died in 1961 at the age of 101, but her work remains popular and is still shown in galleries and art shows today.

Name _____

For Thinking and Discussing

1. Why is Anna Mary Robertson Moses known better as "Grandma Moses"?

   _____

   _____

   _____

   _____

2. Judging from what you know of Grandma Moses, what values did she consider most important?

   _____

   _____

   _____

   _____

3. Anna once said that she didn't ". . . bring up the children, they kind of come up." What did she mean by this statement and how does this view differ from that of most parents of today?

   _____

   _____

   _____

   _____

4. Why did Grandma Moses wait so long in life before she turned to serious painting?

   _____

   _____

   _____

   _____

Name _____

5. Anna Mary Robertson once said in her later years that if she hadn't started painting, she would have raised chickens. How could someone as talented as she have paralleled her paintings with raising chickens?

_____

_____

_____

_____

_____

_____

_____

For Further Research

Find copies of some paintings of Grandma Moses. Look at them carefully, compare them and then describe her work in your own words. What was she trying to say, if anything?

SANDRA DAY O'CONNOR

Sandra Day O'Connor distinguished herself among women in history by becoming the first woman to sit on the U.S. Supreme Court. Her nomination by President Reagan in 1981 and her approval by the U.S. Senate was applauded by women everywhere as one more stride toward equality. She was born in El Paso, Texas, in 1930 and grew up on a 150,000 acre ranch in southeastern Arizona that had been founded by her grandfather. Because her parents felt she was too bright to be educated by the rural schools of the area, they sent her to live with her maternal grandmother in El Paso at the age of five. There she attended Redford School, a private school for girls. She did come back to visit her parents often, and her loneliness for home caused her to spend part of her high school education in Lordsbury (near her home), but that meant boarding the bus before dawn and getting home after dark at night.

After high school she enrolled in Stanford University, where she graduated *magna cum laude* in 1950. She also graduated from Stanford's School of Law in 1952. It was there Sandra Day met her husband-to-be, John Jay O'Connor, another student of law. She tried to get jobs with several Los Angeles and San Francisco law firms, but was turned away because she was a woman. She then turned to public service, working as a deputy attorney in San Mateo, California, while her husband finished law school. The couple then spent three years in West Germany. In 1957 they settled in Maricopa County, Arizona, where she opened her practice. In 1969 she was appointed to fill a vacancy in the state senate and her career in politics began. During her five years in the senate she championed the rights of women. In 1974 she shifted to the judiciary department winning a hard-fought battle for a judgeship. In 1979 she was appointed to serve on the Arizona Court of Appeals. Her moderate views and conservatism made her a politically attractive candidate. When he campaigned for the presidency, Ronald Reagan incurred much resentment from women because of his opposition to the ERA. He thus vowed to fill the first vacancy in the Supreme Court with the most qualified woman. His search ended with Sandra Day O'Connor. Although her appointment was eventually approved by the Senate, there were several opponents who voiced their opposition during the confirmation hearings. It was her split with basic Republican values on abortion that caused most of the opposition, but when the final vote was taken, she was approved by ninety-one U.S. senators.

Name _____

For Thinking and Discussing

1. How would Sandra Day O'Connor's early experience in riding a bus to school have helped to make her an opponent against busing?

_____

_____

_____

_____

2. As a state legislator, Sandra Day O'Connor was very much concerned with fighting discrimination against women. Why do you think this was such a major issue with her?

_____

_____

_____

_____

3. Why did Ronald Reagan launch an all out search in 1981 to find a woman to replace Justice Potter Stewart, when he retired from the U.S. Supreme Court?

_____

_____

_____

_____

4. On July 7, 1981, Ronald Reagan announced that his search for the "most qualified woman" was over. He had found "Sandra Day O'Connor, truly a person for all seasons." What did Reagan mean by this statement?

_____

_____

_____

_____

Name _____

5. Although she was approved for the appointment to the Supreme Court, there was a certain amount of opposition that surfaced during the confirmation hearings. Most of it centered around her alleged ''lack of respect for traditional family values.'' What complaint against Sandra Day O'Connor were these opponents raising?

_____

_____

_____

_____

_____

_____

_____

For Further Research

One of the reasons Ronald Reagan chose Sandra Day O'Connor to fill the vacancy on the Supreme Court was her opinion on how the federal, state and local courts should function. This opinion was in accord with his own. Find out her judicial philosophy on how the court system at these various levels should work.

JACQUELINE KENNEDY ONASSIS

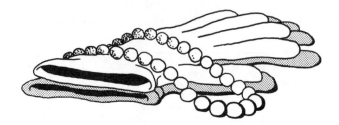

Perhaps the most glamorous of First Ladies was Mrs. John F. Kennedy, who made her mark in history not because of her political power but because of her beauty and charm and impeccable good taste for the finer things in life. Her power lay in her sense of style, and the complete refurbishing of the White House she did during her husband's administration was applauded by the entire nation. Her proud and stoic behavior during the days following the tragic assassination of President Kennedy presented her to America as a truly remarkable woman. Jackie grew up the complete cosmopolitan. Her youth centered around summers at Easthampton and winters on Park Avenue. Her education was likewise first class, with such prestigious fashionable schools as Miss Chapin's School in New York, Miss Porter's School in Connecticut, Vassar, the University of Grenoble, Sorbonne and George Washington Universities.

She became the Inquiring Camera Girl for the *Washington Times-Herald* before her association with John F. Kennedy, who was then a U.S. Senator. She conducted an interview with him and the couple developed a fashionable courtship. When they married, the affair was indeed a gala and unsurprisingly one of the really big social events of the year. In her role as First Lady she did not welcome the publicity, but she seemed to cause a sensation at whatever she did. She became noted for her entertainment of foreign leaders, receiving seventy-four during the first two years of Kennedy's administration. She was always well-briefed in advance on the leader or dignitary she would be receiving, and her lavish flair for entertaining left an indelible impression on their minds.

She also indulged her taste for the fine arts bringing classical music, ballet and the theater to the White House. She stayed pretty much out of politics, especially when she was pregnant with her third child during the Kennedy administration. But when the baby died, she became a willing traveler with Jack and accompanied him on his ill-fated trip to Dallas. The strength and courage she summoned during the hours after the assassination etched her image further into the public consciousness. In 1968 she married the wealthy Aristotle Onassis, a man who was twenty-five years her senior. "Jackie-O" became one of the fast-moving "jet-set" surrounded by maids and servants, and she lost many of her following. But she will always be remembered historically as the First Lady who brought glamor to the White House.

Name _____

For Thinking and Discussing

1. Jacqueline Kennedy once said, ''I want to make the White House the most perfect house in America.'' She then set out to do that very thing. What was included in this ''restoration'' that was approved by the entire nation?

    _____

    _____

    _____

    _____

2. Famous designer of women's clothing Edith Head once called Jackie Kennedy the greatest single influence on fashion in history. How and why was she such a style setter?

    _____

    _____

    _____

    _____

3. How did Jacqueline Kennedy's background serve her well as the most glamorous of First Ladies?

    _____

    _____

    _____

    _____

4. The Kennedys' hosting of foreign leaders and diplomats became almost legend. Aside from the fact that they entertained a great number, how did Jackie help to make this phase of the Kennedy administration memorable and famous?

    _____

    _____

    _____

    _____

Name _____

5. No First Lady, aside from Eleanor Roosevelt, ever so impressed the world as did Jacqueline Kennedy. How did she do this without paying much heed to the political arena?

_____

_____

_____

_____

_____

_____

_____

_____

For Further Research

The stoic yet graceful manner in which Jacqueline Kennedy dealt with the aftermath of her husband's assassination created an image on America and the world that would never be forgotten. Find out the things she did and the way she handled the tragedy that created this lasting impression.

EMILY POST

Her name has come to mean "the proper thing to do." Emily Post has been declared by acclaim the dictator of correct behavior. Her unique niche in history was made by a combination of the lofty social position she held and her 1922 best-seller *Etiquette* which caught on immediately and has been accepted as the authority on manners ever since.

She was born in Baltimore, Maryland, in 1873, to parents who were not only wealthy, but also were high atop the social ladder of the day. Emily was five years old when her family moved to New York City. Her childhood was one of those where everything fell into the "acceptable and proper" way of being raised. As she grew older her education included trips abroad.

Her debut in 1892 was indeed one of the social events of the year, complete with fashionable parties and gala ball celebrations. In the end it was the flamboyant Edwin Post, a wealthy New York banker, who won her hand in marriage. The couple continued to live in the same fashionable cafe society to which they were both accustomed, until 1901, when Post lost his money. There followed a divorce and Emily Price Post (the name she chose to use after her divorce, making her the first divorcee to do so) suddenly was without a substantial income. She was urged by friends toward a career in writing, even though such work was considered below the social rung to which she had been reared. Her first published book was a novel called *The Flight of the Moth.*

It was Richard Duffy of Funk and Wagnall, who first suggested she write a book on etiquette. She despised the idea, but he convinced her by giving her a book on the subject by another writer. Post read the book and went to work the next morning on her book, *Etiquette*, which became an immediate best-seller. Its success was attributed to her background and position in society and her emphasizing that good manners are based mostly on good common sense. She revised the book several times to account for changes in social conditions. Her career mushroomed into a syndicated daily newspaper column and radio broadcasts on her advice. Even though she was a very busy lady with all her interests, Emily Post was never too busy to answer the "special problems" in the volume of mail she received. She died in 1960, but her advice, with updates for societal change, is still popular today.

Name _____

For Thinking and Discussing

1. How did the childhood environment provided for Emily Post by her parents help prepare her for her spot in history?

   _____

   _____

   _____

   _____

2. Why did Edwin Post, a wealthy New York banker, seem to be a perfect husband for Emily Price?

   _____

   _____

   _____

   _____

3. What influence did Richard Duffy have on the writing career of Emily Post and how did her writing change with his influence?

   _____

   _____

   _____

   _____

4. Even though she despised the idea of writing a book on etiquette, Duffy was able to convince her she was the right person for the job. How did he do this?

   _____

   _____

   _____

   _____

Name _____

5. Why was her book so widely acclaimed and what was her basic philosophy on appropriate behavior and good manners?

_____

_____

_____

_____

_____

_____

_____

_____

For Further Research

Emily Post's book *Etiquette* is still regarded as *the* authority on good manners, even though she died in 1960. The book has been reprinted several times and remains the top seller among such books. Obtain a copy of a recent edition and jot down a list of appropriate behaviors you did not know before.

SALLY RIDE

On June 18, 1983, Sally Ride became the first American woman to fly in space. She insisted throughout her training that she was not in the astronaut program as a symbol of the feminist movement nor for any other reason than the fact that she wanted to fly in space. She was nevertheless an overnight celebrity and became a focal point of those women who were involved in achieving feminine equality. She was born in 1951 in Encino, California, the daughter of a professor at Santa Monica Community College. Sally's parents did not put pressure on her and her sister, but they provided them the opportunity to expand their minds. Sally began playing tennis when she was ten and became an excellent tennis player, at one time ranking 18th nationally among juniors. She won a tennis scholarship to Westlake School for Girls, and there she met Dr. Elizabeth Mommaerts, her physiology instructor, who would influence her toward a life in science. After Westlake, Sally enrolled at Swarthmore College, but dropped out after three semesters to work on her tennis game. After three months of hard work, she decided she wasn't good enough to become a professional, so she went back to college—this time enrolling at Stanford University. She received both her B.A. and B.S. degrees there in 1973 and then began working on a doctorate in astrophysics. While she was working on her dissertation, she began looking for a job in research physics. She read the announcement by NASA about their search for "mission specialists," and she applied along with 8,000 others! To her surprise Sally survived the preliminary round and became one of the finalists flown to Houston to the Lyndon B. Johnson Space Center. Three months later, Sally Ride became an astronaut. She then began the intensive training that includes parachute jumping, flying a jet and acclimating her body to increased g force.

In 1982 Captain Robert L. Crippen, commander of the seventh scheduled shuttle mission, personally chose Sally Ride to be a member of his crew. Her role was to serve as flight engineer as well as mission specialist. The purpose of the mission was to test a 50-foot remote controlled mechanical arm that could retrieve satellites and other space payloads. Dr. Ride performed her assigned tasks to perfection. During the ceremonies and hoopla that followed, Sally Ride was the focus of attention, but she declined all invitations that did not include all members of the crew. In July 1982, Sally Ride married Steven A. Hawley, an astronomer and fellow astronaut.

Name _____

For Thinking and Discussing

1. Even though Sally Ride tried to make it very clear that she became an astronaut because she wanted to fly in space and not to achieve any feminist goals, she nevertheless became an instant celebrity among women. Why do you suppose this happened?

   _____

   _____

   _____

   _____

2. Why did NASA lift its ban on allowing women in the space program?

   _____

   _____

   _____

   _____

3. How did Sally Ride decide between seeking a career as a tennis player and going back to college?

   _____

   _____

   _____

   _____

4. Why did Navy Captain Robert L. Crippen, commander of the seventh space shuttle mission, choose Sally Ride?

   _____

   _____

   _____

   _____

Name _____

5. When Sally Ride's trip into space had ended, NASA was deluged with requests to use her name and image on posters, T-shirts, and other commercial merchandise. NASA declined all such requests. Why?

_____

_____

_____

_____

_____

_____

_____

For Further Research

When Captain Robert L. Crippen chose Sally Ride for his mission, he wasn't just choosing her because she was a woman. She was in his own words, ''The best person for the job.'' Find out her specific tasks performed during the mission and why she was especially well-qualified.

ELEANOR ROOSEVELT

Eleanor Roosevelt was perhaps the most influential of all President's wives. She was also the most criticized and the most revered of First Ladies, with her power and influence deep and lasting. But she was not a feminist and she deplored any emphasis on sex differentiation in the political arena. She denied any influence over her husband on political affairs. But who could deny that she was a force to be reckoned with. She was subjected to personal abuse by both women and men for her homely features, her high-pitched voice and her views, but she basically ignored their criticism and forged ahead.

Although she was born into a privileged family, she made an early commitment to political activism and helping the poor. Mrs. Roosevelt was deeply involved in all the big causes of her time and devoted special attention to social inequality. She was idolized by Blacks and broke with the Daughters of the American Revolution because they once closed Constitution Hall to Marian Anderson, a famous black singer. Her following played a large role in swinging millions of black votes to the Democratic Party, a move that shows that trend yet today.

She credits her political education to Louis Howe, her husband's advisor, who constantly encouraged both of them and masterminded the Roosevelt political campaign. When Franklin was stricken with a disabling disease, it was Howe and Eleanor who convinced him to return to full-scale political life. Although she supported Franklin's every move and served as his constant advice, she did not particularly relish the role of being First Lady. The country was deeply entrenched in the Great Depression, and the steps taken by her husband to solve the many problems took Eleanor to all parts of the world and caused her a great deal of personal sacrifice. But she weathered all storms and became totally committed to the programs of her husband's New Deal. She served in the capacity of First Lady longer than anyone else, since her husband died shortly after being elected to an unprecedented fourth term of office. She was then appointed as the United States delegate to the United Nations, a position to which she brought dignity and prestige. She also threw her heart into support of the Democratic Party and fought for Adlai Stevenson in his 1952 and 1956 bids to become President. When she died in November of 1962, her death was mourned all over the world by countless people who had better times because of her.

Name _____

For Thinking and Discussing

1. There were millions of people who considered Eleanor Roosevelt one of the greatest women in history. There were others who disliked her a great deal. Why would someone with such a profound personality be the subject of such personal abuse and criticism?

_____
_____
_____
_____

2. How did she overcome her handicap of speaking in public with an uncontrollable, high-pitched giggle that destroyed the effectiveness of her serious messages?

_____
_____
_____
_____

3. How is Eleanor Roosevelt credited with bringing millions of loyal black votes to the Democratic Party?

_____
_____
_____
_____

4. Who exerted the most influence in creating the political fire and spirit that was so much a part of Eleanor Roosevelt?

_____
_____
_____

Name _____

5. Although Eleanor Roosevelt did many things to influence and encourage equal rights for women, she also helped the cause of Blacks. Describe the incident with the famous black singer Marian Anderson which made her a hero among Blacks.

_____

_____

_____

_____

_____

_____

_____

For Further Research

Eleanor Roosevelt was indeed an amazing woman. Her special interests and accomplishments were only briefly touched in the biographical sketch. Research from other sources and list in detail the achievements of this very special woman.

DIANA ROSS

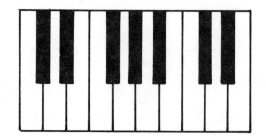

The "Motown Sound" of the Supremes led by Diana Ross created a new dimension in black pop music and caught on in popularity with whites as well. Their more than 12,000,000 records sold during the '60's was second only to the Beatles. When she broke away from the group, her success story continued and she reached a new popularity when cast as Billie Holiday in the movie *Lady Sings the Blues.*

She was born in 1944 in a low-income housing project in Detroit. She had two sisters and three brothers, who all slept in the same room. Diana's name had been misspelled on her birth certificate and should have been more properly spelled *Diane.* Continuing a family tradition, she sang in the choir at the Olivet Baptist Church where her grandfather was minister. After high school she worked as a bus girl in the cafeteria of a Detroit department store. Diana and two friends, Florence Ballard and Mary Wilson, began singing semiprofessionally under the name of the Primettes. In 1959 the group was introduced to Berry Gordy, who was in the process of marketing a new recording company called Motown—a contraction of *motor* and *town*—the name often used in making reference to Detroit. Gordy used the group at first as background singers for Marvin Gaye and the Shirelles. As he groomed them for stardom, he changed their name from the Primettes to the Supremes. Their first nine singles weren't very successful, so Gordy hired a new team of writers to tailor songs especially for them. They finally hit it big with "Where Did Our Love Go?" in 1964 and followed up with five more Gold Records, thus becoming the first group to have six Gold Records.

After several more Gold Records and years of success, Diana Ross announced she was going to pursue a career on her own. Her nightclub act was an immediate success with her salary ranging upward of $25,000 a week. Her Motown roots gave her a sound that was both lyrical and unique and made her a star. But critics described her as being the "total entertainer," not merely because of her voice but also because of her vitality and her stage presence. Her performances were hailed as "electric."

She made her film debut in 1972 with *Lady Sing the Blues.* Although the movie received less than satisfactory reviews, the acting ability of Diana Ross was applauded as a new talent that would take her far in motion pictures. In 1970 she was named Female Entertainer of the Year. In 1971 she married public relations executive Robert Ellis Silberstein.

Name _____

For Thinking and Discussing

1. What evidence can you find from the childhood of Diana Ross that could have contributed to her success as a singer and entertainer?

_____

_____

_____

_____

2. How did Diana Ross and the Supremes get their start as a group?

_____

_____

_____

_____

3. How did Berry Gordy take the Supremes from a trio of backup singers to fame and stardom and records that sold millions of copies?

_____

_____

_____

_____

4. What is the significance of a Gold Record?

_____

_____

_____

_____

Name _____

5. To what should we attribute the overwhelming success of Diana Ross as a solo entertainer once she broke away from the Supremes?

_____

_____

_____

_____

_____

_____

_____

_____

For Further Research

The career of Diana Ross as an entertainer is far from over. Trace her accomplishments and successes from the mid '70's to the present.

SACAGAWEA

Sacagawea was the Shoshoni Indian woman who guided Meriwether Lewis and William Clark on their famous exploration of the West. It was during the administration of Thomas Jefferson that a number of Americans became interested in learning about what lay ahead west of the Mississippi River. Rumors and stories aroused the curiosity of Jefferson to the point that he decided to do something about it. Even though the United States didn't own the land, he convinced Congress to appropriate funds for an exploring expedition. Before the trip was finalized, Jefferson had bought from France the vast land called Louisiana. This huge tract of land extended from New Orleans north to Canada and west from the Mississippi River to the Continental Divide.

The party commissioned to explore the vast region was headed by the Virginians Meriwether Lewis and William Clark. The party also included a French-Canadian trapper Toussaint Charbonneau, his Indian wife Sacagawea and their infant son Jean Baptiste. He was hired as the interpreter and his wife had been taken captive, sold as a slave and eventually became his property. His bringing her along on the journey proved to be a more than wise decision. She was the only woman among some forty men who made the 8,000-mile trek, and her presence alone was a sign of peace to the many tribes of Indians they encountered along the way. When food became scarce, she hunted for plants and herbs that were edible. There are many accounts of her resourcefulness proving highly valuable to the well-being of the entire expedition. She also convinced her own tribe, the Lenshi Shoshoni Indians, to provide the expedition with horses and to direct the group to the Columbia River. Journals tell of her desire to see the Pacific Ocean and ''that monstrous fish'' (whale) and of how Clark granted her permission to be included in the final expedition that went to the ''great stinking pond'' in 1806. The party returned to Fort Mandan (in present North Dakota) on August 17, 1806, some two years and four months after they had departed. Then Sacagawea, her husband and their son, who had been nicknamed Pompey by the group, departed from the group. But Clark did not forget Sacagawea and wrote in his accounts of the trip of the courage and the value she had been on the long and dangerous journey. There are conflicting accounts of her death with one source saying she died in 1812. A separate account has her surviving until 1884.

Name _____

For Thinking and Discussing

1. How did Sacagawea prove to be so valuable to the Lewis and Clark expedition?

   _____

   _____

   _____

   _____

2. Although the party was interested in studying the flora and fauna as well as the land itself, what was the main concern of the Lewis and Clark expedition?

   _____

   _____

   _____

   _____

   _____

3. Why is the Louisiana Purchase considered to be one of "the great property" deals of all time?

   _____

   _____

   _____

   _____

   _____

4. What were the boundaries of the vast tract of land called Louisiana, land that literally doubled the size of the United States overnight?

   _____

   _____

   _____

   _____

Name _____

5. What did Lewis and Clark have to report of their journey that covered 8,000 miles and lasted well over two years?

_____

_____

_____

_____

_____

_____

_____

_____

For Further Research

Although Jefferson had long been interested in what was west of the Mississippi River, the actual purchase of Louisiana was almost by chance happening. He initially wanted to buy only New Orleans and surrounding territory. Find out why this was ''necessary'' and how the United States was able to buy all of Louisiana instead.

BEVERLY SILLS

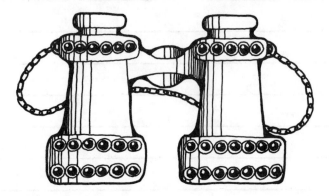

Beverly Sills represents one of the truly gratifying success stories of American opera. Her talent as an opera singer for twenty-five years culminated in 1979 with her announcement of retirement as a singer to become the director of the New York City Opera. The story of her lifelong ambition of running a major opera company clearly identifies the ups and downs she faced in realizing her goal.

She was born Belle Miriam Silverman in 1929, the daughter of a successful real estate broker. At birth her doctor noticed a bubble in her mouth. He broke the bubble and nicknamed her "Bubbly"—a name she carried through her years. Her parents were convinced of her talent at a very early age and provided her with voice and dance lessons. In 1936 she auditioned before Estelle Liebling, her voice coach who remained both her professional and personal friend until her death in 1970. Liebling encouraged Beverly to interview for CBS radio's "Major Bowes' Amateur Hour." As a result she began playing the role of Elaine Raleigh on the radio soap opera "Our Gal Sunday" and did commercials for Rinso White. She "retired" at the age of twelve and resumed a normal childhood, but in 1945, she launched a full-time career under the guidance of Broadway producer J.J. Schubert, who was determined to make her a star. She eventually landed the role of Baby in *The Ballad of Baby Doe,* when she proved herself as a promising young soprano.

In 1956 she married Peter Buckeley Greenough, the wealthy editor of the Cleveland *Plain Dealer.* Their two children ("Muffy" and "Bucky") both had handicaps that caused Beverly to retire from her career ". . . because she had other things on her mind." But she eventually overcame her bitterness and returned to the New York City Opera. Her role as Cleopatra was the turning point in her career. The years that followed solidified her position as a virtuoso soprano. One of the proudest aspects of her career was that she proved herself a success, without the Metropolitan Opera. Finally, in 1975, she appeared there as Pamira in *The Siege of Corinth* and received an eighteen-minute ovation for her performance. In 1980, she announced her retirement to become the co-director of the New York City Opera. Her farewell to the American public was October 27, 1980, when she appeared at Lincoln Center in a fund-raising event that raised over a million dollars for the New York City Opera.

Name _____

For Thinking and Discussing

1. What early influences did Beverly Sills have that headed her life toward a career in opera?

   _____
   _____
   _____
   _____

2. After her marriage to Peter Buckeley Greenough and the birth of two children, Beverly Sills temporarily retired, saying she had "other things on her mind." What caused this change of heart?

   _____
   _____
   _____
   _____

3. What was the turning point in the career of Beverly Sills?

   _____
   _____
   _____
   _____

4. What does Beverly Sills consider to be the crowning achievement of her operatic career?

   _____
   _____
   _____
   _____

Name _____

5. Why was Beverly Sills so proud of the fact that she was a ''revolutionary''?

_____

_____

_____

_____

_____

_____

_____

_____

For Further Research

Before she became an accepted star of opera, Beverly Sills' career as a singer was filled with less than spectacular roles. However, they all added up to exposure and could be said to be contributing factors to her success. Trace her career from her first appearance on ''Uncle Bob's Radio House'' to her role of Cleopatra in *Julius Caesar*.

MARGARET CHASE SMITH

Margaret Chase Smith was the first woman to be elected to and serve in both the United States House of Representatives and the United States Senate. She was known as the Quiet Woman because she rarely spoke in the Senate. Yet she was not a quiet person when it came to getting involved. She was the center of much controversy and conflict. Her husband Clyde Smith was serving in the House of Representatives in 1940 when he suffered a major heart attack. His doctor advised his wife Maggie to complete his term. He had another attack and died shortly after she accepted the appointment. She then served four two-year terms in the House before being elected to the United States Senate in 1948. She was reelected three times and served in the Senate from 1949 to 1973. Her life-style remained a simple yet efficient routine of rising early, exercising, eating a light breakfast, driving to her office, where she usually ate lunch and remained working till around six o'clock. She then took letters home with her to work on until she fell asleep.

Because she developed a reputation as a lady who said little, people listened closely when she did choose to speak. Her famous Declaration of Conscience speech, which openly attacked the tactics of fellow Senator Joseph McCarthy, supported her untiring belief in the principles of Americanism—namely the right to uphold unpopular beliefs, the right to protest and the right to think free and independent thoughts. She was warned not to make the speech, and she left herself open to criticism by those who supported McCarthy. But she stood by her principles and was asked to serve on the committee that investigated McCarthy and eventually censured his actions. She was widely known as one of the most well-informed of U.S. Senators, and she has consistently ranked in polls as one of the top ten Senators. Her attendance record also stands out. She once was honored for voting 2,000 consecutive times without a miss! Her courage, her dedication and her integrity made her one of the most influential legislators in Washington. The record-breaking mandates she received from the voters of Maine are testament to the respect she earned from others. Her autobiography is called *Declaration of Conscience*.

Name _____

For Thinking and Discussing

1. How did Margaret Chase Smith first become a member of Congress?

   _____
   _____
   _____
   _____

2. What do you think Margaret Chase Smith would think of Geraldine Ferraro's unsuccessful attempt to win the vice presidency in 1984?

   _____
   _____
   _____
   _____

3. Margaret Chase Smith never hesitated to bring down the giants whenever she felt they were wrong. She often did this at the risk of personal censure and widespread criticism. What causes people to subject themselves to such controversy?

   _____
   _____
   _____
   _____

4. What was the meaning of Margaret Smith's "Kennedy Twist"—the term she used in criticizing President Kennedy?

   _____
   _____
   _____
   _____

Name _____

5. Why was Senator Smith so outspoken against fellow Senator Joseph McCarthy?

_____

_____

_____

_____

_____

_____

_____

_____

For Further Research

The "Quiet Woman" was anything but quiet when she felt the need to stand up for her beliefs and criticize those she felt were in the wrong. Aside from her attack on Joseph McCarthy, what other "attacks" did she launch during her tenure in office?

GLORIA STEINEM

Gloria Steinem, with her lectures and provocative articles, has become one of the most active feminists in the current movement toward equality for women. What she observed and heard during her travels in the early 1970's gave her the confidence that there was an adequate audience in America that was waiting for a magazine totally for, by and about women. Thus in 1972 she co-founded *Ms.* magazine. It soon became the national forum for women seeking true equality with men.

Steinem was born in Toledo, Ohio, in 1934 and graduated from Smith College in 1956. Her early career included television writing and working as an editor and consultant for magazines like *The Ladies' Home Journal* and *Seventeen.* Gloria Steinem became actively involved in the feminist movement in 1968. She feels that her efforts have been well worthwhile because they have led to action. One of her main themes throughout her writing and speaking has been that people should indeed cherish the individuality of other individuals. If this were true, there would be no need for a feminist movement. She began speaking as a team with Dorothy Pitman Hughes to small groups of women in places like shopping malls and parking lots. At first the reaction to feminists' teams was one of novelty, but the movement began to gain strength in the early 1970's and it soon became a national feeling. The couple toured the entire country, focusing on the problems and inequality of women. As the movement grew, so did the opposition, and the pair were victims of harassment and abuse on many occasions.

When Steinem became the focus of national attention, she was often asked to speak before large groups of people and to serve as a guest on major talk shows. She had a problem of being extremely nervous during such occasions, and her pulse would become very rapid and her mouth would go dry. She turned down many invitations because of the inability to speak before large groups of people. But Steinem worked very hard to overcome her problem and eventually became the profound, impressive public speaker she is today. Gloria Steinem began with the idea her work would last only a few years. She would point out the inequalities, and they would be cured. Obviously, things didn't work out that way—and even though women have made giant strides since Gloria Steinem began, her work goes on—simply because there is so much more to do.

Name _____

For Thinking and Discussing

1. Why do you think Gloria Steinem became involved in the feminist movement to strive for the equality of all mankind?

   _____

   _____

   _____

   _____

2. In 1971, Gloria Steinem helped to establish the National Women's Political Caucus. What are the main goals and objectives of this organization?

   _____

   _____

   _____

   _____

3. What was Gloria Steinem's main reason for founding *Ms.* magazine and how did it differ from other magazines for women?

   _____

   _____

   _____

   _____

4. Why did Gloria Steinem oftentimes turn down invitations to appear on talk shows when her main goal was to gain an audience who would listen to her views on women's rights?

   _____

   _____

   _____

   _____

Name _____

5. How did Steinem overcome her fear of speaking before large groups of people?

_____

_____

_____

_____

_____

_____

_____

_____

For Further Research

Through the years Gloria Steinem has come to several realizations in her talks and travels about how women can effectively deal with the problems associated with inequality. Research from another source her strategy on how women can best be heard and effectively work toward their goals.

LUCY STONE

Lucy Stone was one of the foremost leaders in the movement to advance the rights of women in the United States. Her lectures on antislavery and women's rights combined with her fire and determination to succeed made her one of the most outspoken women of her day. As a young child she had been disturbed at the long hours of drudgery imposed on her mother, and she rejected the biblical stand that men should rule over women. As she once said, "There was only one will in our house and that was my father's." In fact her mother had milked eight cows the night before Lucy's birth.

When she married Henry Blackwell, she insisted on keeping her maiden name, and she wrote out one of the first "marriage contracts" ever. Lucy also insisted that the word *obey* be deleted from the marriage vows. She had been so determined to go to college that she scrimped and saved her money for nine years to get enough money to enter Oberlin College in Ohio at the age of twenty-five. Because she had to take in extra jobs to support her education expenses, she would rise at 2:00 in the morning to study. Her outspoken views made her somewhat unpopular with members of the faculty, but she graduated at the head of her class in 1847, becoming one of the first women in the United States to earn a college degree. Her degree was in jeopardy for awhile as she was invited to write an essay for commencement exercises, but was not going to be allowed to read the essay. She considered it an insult and refused to write the essay.

Such was the life-style of Lucy Stone, who lectured throughout the United States and Canada relating to all who would listen of the evils of slavery and discrimination against women. She did her best to convince her good friend Antoinette Brown not to marry because she feared "Nette" would allow her husband to rule the marriage. The two eventually became sisters-in-law when they married the Blackwell brothers. Lucy Stone, however insisted on the marriage contract, and she spelled out the independence as a human being she expected from her husband.

Lucy Stone was one of the first women to speak out on the injustice of preventing women from voting. Although she died in 1893, long before women actually won the right to vote, she was proud of the success she had achieved, even though the "price to pay had been great."

Name _____

For Thinking and Discussing

1. Why do you think Lucy Stone insisted on keeping her maiden name of Stone when she married Henry Blackwell, even though the arrangement placed both of them under ridicule by the public?

   _____

   _____

   _____

   _____

2. Lucy Stone was one of four "friends" who together waged many battles and crusades down through the years, even though they didn't always agree and in fact split in their views and support of issues several times. Who were the other three "contemporaries"?

   _____

   _____

3. During her close friendship with Antoinette Brown at Oberlin College, Lucy Stone argued with "Nette" against ever getting married. Why do you think she took this position and tried to convince others of the same?

   _____

   _____

   _____

   _____

   _____

4. What would Lucy Stone think of a woman running for President of the United States?

   _____

   _____

   _____

   _____

   _____

Name _____

5. What advice do you think Lucy Stone would give her thirteen-year-old daughter today?

_____

_____

_____

_____

_____

_____

_____

_____

For Further Research

Lucy Stone was one of the founders of the American Woman Suffrage Association, which became one of the leading women's associations in the country. Find out about its successes, its failures, and the frustration it experienced down through the years.

HARRIET BEECHER STOWE

Harriet Beecher Stowe was born the daughter of an orthodox Calvinist minister who preached fiery sermons on the horrors of hellfire. He infused in his children his burning desire to reform mankind. Harriet grew up listening to her father speak in pulpit tones (even though he wasn't in the pulpit at the time) of the consecration of man, and his lofty goals and value system had a strong impact on her. She grew up feeling that she was constantly falling short of his expectations and felt herself so unworthy she even once said she hoped she would die young that she might " . . . take her faults to an early grave . . . ."

In 1832 her father became president of Lane Theological Seminary in Cincinnati, where Harriet met Calvin Stowe, a professor of the classics, whom she married. Stowe was fussy and tyrannical, and he treated Harriet like a servant. His mother even moved in with the couple. Then after ten years of marriage, which produced three children, she developed a mysterious paralysis of her right side. She was admitted to a sanitarium in Vermont to take a "water cure" for her paralysis. During her time there she faithfully wrote daily to her helpless husband, who constantly complained of his life with the children and his mother. The peace and calm of the sanitarium was like a balm to Harriet, who enjoyed life like she never had before.

After stretching her visit into months, she and her family were reunited, with her husband taking a position at Bowdoin College. It was in New Brunswick, Maine, that Harriet wrote *Uncle Tom's Cabin.* She began writing the novel to portray how the institution of slavery was destroying family life. The novel was serialized in the abolitionist paper *The National Era,* and she intended for it to be three or four installments in length. But its immense popularity caused her to ramble on to forty before she was finished. Its impact was overwhelming, with the book being by far the most important and most popular book of the nineteenth century, selling over 500,000 copies in the United States alone before it was translated into more than twenty foreign languages. Though certainly not a great literary work, it formed a national conscience on the issue of slavery, and it stands historically as perhaps the most significant single book in American history. Harriet Beecher Stowe also believed strongly in the reform for women and wrote a manual on housekeeping for women. In the book she advanced the theme of a good Christian home being the result of a woman taking charge in many situations.

Name _____

For Thinking and Discussing

1. How would Harriet's father Lyman have been a guiding force in her eventual writing of *Uncle Tom's Cabin*?

   _____

   _____

   _____

   _____

2. Why do you think Harriet Beecher Stowe stretched her stay at Brattleboro Sanitarium into several months, even though it meant being away from her family?

   _____

   _____

   _____

3. She was originally scheduled to write only "three to four installments" of the work for *The National Era.* Why was the book stretched to forty?

   _____

   _____

   _____

4. Historians often point to the book *Uncle Tom's Cabin* as one of the causes of the Civil War. In fact Abraham Lincoln said to Stowe when she visited him, "Is this the little woman who made the great war?" How could a book have such a powerful impact on society?

   _____

   _____

   _____

   _____

Name _____

5. How did Harriet Beecher Stowe help to advance the cause of women?

_____

_____

_____

_____

_____

_____

_____

_____

For Further Research

Read *Uncle Tom's Cabin* and find out how the incidents of the author's life helped to contribute to the story that unfolds.

BARBRA STREISAND

Barbra Streisand continues today to have one of the most successful singing and acting careers in the history of the entertainment business. From the Gold Records to the Academy Awards she's won to the honored appearances she has made, Barbra Streisand has left that indelible quality called charisma that has made her a star.

She was born in Brooklyn, New York, and grew up on Flatbush Avenue, a ghetto of run-down shacks and graffiti-covered buildings. Her father held a Ph.D. in education and held high hopes for his family when his second child, Barbra was born. Fifteen months later he suffered a brain hemorrhage and died, leaving his family without an adequate source of income. Though she never consciously knew her father, subconsciously she set her standards of perfection on what she thought he would want them to be, and there is also doubt she would have been the fighter she became in her rise to stardom had she been reared in the environment of love and reassurance and material comfort her father would have provided.

At Erasmus High, where she graduated with straight A's, she became acutely aware of the jokes about her looks and big nose. She tried various types of makeup and fantasized her life in the role of several stars of the day, but somehow she just didn't fit. By throwing out the rules of fashion, she created an offbeat new and refreshing look that was soon to be copied by others. The result was that she became beautiful to others because she acted beautiful. Over her years of success, Barbra developed a bad rapport with the news media and created several "scenes" of bad temper during the filming of her movies. Her critics called it ego; Barbra preferred to call it her strive for perfection. Her list of accomplishments should be testament enough for this goal. At the age of twenty-seven, she had become the only person—male or female, to have won a Tony Award for theatre, a Grammy for recording, an Emmy for television, and an Oscar for motion pictures. Her story has the makings of an ugly duckling turned into a swan, but she did it all on her own terms and she did it her way. Her award-winning performance as Fanny Brice in *Funny Girl* said a lot about her own life, and her amazing string of successes that followed in *Hello Dolly!* and *The Way We Were* led her to box office fame that commanded $4 million a picture.

Name _____

For Thinking and Discussing

1. How did the death of Barbra Streisand's father (when she was only fifteen months old) have an eventual result on her becoming a star?

   _____

   _____

   _____

   _____

2. It almost goes without saying that part of the reason for the successful career of Barbra Streisand lies in her charismatic charm. Describe this charisma that has helped to win her so many fans.

   _____

   _____

   _____

   _____

3. How did Barbra Streisand turn the disadvantage of her big nose and rather homely looks into an asset?

   _____

   _____

   _____

   _____

4. Why did Barbra develop a bad relationship with the media and a reputation among movie producers as a woman who was very difficult to deal with?

   _____

   _____

   _____

   _____

Name _____

5. List some of the box office smashes that allowed Barbra Streisand to command a salary of $4 million per picture.

_____

_____

_____

_____

_____

_____

_____

_____

For Further Research

At the age of twenty-seven, Barbra Streisand became the only person, male or female, to have won every major entertainment award. She won a Tony Award, an Emmy Award, a Grammy award, and an Oscar. Find out the areas of entertainment for which these awards are given and then, more specifically, what she won the award for in each case.

HARRIET TUBMAN

Harriet Tubman was a black slave who escaped herself, then helped others to escape to freedom in Canada or the free states. She was the leader of the underground railroad, the famous network of secret hiding places, food stops and directional help created to help slaves escape to the north. She was known as Moses after the biblical figure who had led his people out of captivity in Egypt. She was born a slave named Araminta Ross, but became Harriet (after her mother) in her youth. When she was thirteen, she tried to help save a slave from a white overseer, and he became so enraged he broke her skull with a 2-pound weight. Although she survived, she suffered blackouts the rest of her life. She later married John Tubman, a freed slave. Harriet made her escape from slavery in 1849 and went to Pennsylvania, where slavery was forbidden.

When Congress passed the Fugitive Slave Law, which made it more difficult for slaves to escape, she returned several times into the South to help lead others out of bondage. In fact the best evidence gathered estimates she provided aid and personal direction as she led nearly 300 slaves to freedom in the North. She became so notorious in her efforts that rewards for her capture totaled almost $40,000. Although she was never caught, she experienced several close calls. Because of the total commitment to the cause, she carried a gun threatening to use it on anyone who disobeyed her direction and tried to turn back. It is said that Harriet Tubman, at great personal risk to her own safety, led nineteen such missions. She considered the abolitionist John Brown the true liberator of the slaves. During the Civil War she served as a scout for the Union Army, where she helped free more than 750 slaves during one military campaign. She also served in the capacity of cook, nurse, and spy for the Union Army.

After the war, she opened a home for indigent aged Negroes at her residence in Auburn, New York. It became more popularly known as the Harriet Tubman Home. The people of Auburn erected a plaque in her honor. Her efforts to raise money for black schools was also untiring, and she became active in the women's rights movement during her later years.

In 1978 the United States Post Office issued a stamp bearing her portrait. The stamp commemorated her courage and bravery in leading so many Blacks to their freedom.

Name _____

For Thinking and Discussing

1. What was she called by her people and why?

   _____

   _____

   _____

   _____

2. Even though she escaped to freedom herself, Harriet Tubman returned many times to the dangers and risks of helping fellow Blacks to escape to freedom. She became so notorious for her efforts that there were rewards totalling $40,000 for her capture. Why would she place herself in such personal peril?

   _____

   _____

   _____

   _____

3. The underground railroad was really no railroad at all, but rather a network of secret routes, hiding places, and food stops to aid slaves escaping to Canada. The railroad only operated at night, mainly for two reasons. What were they?

   _____

   _____

   _____

   _____

4. Why did Harriet Tubman suffer from blackouts throughout her adult life?

   _____

   _____

   _____

   _____

Name _____

5. Harriet Tubman is historically remembered for her untiring devotion to freeing Blacks from slavery. How do you think she would feel about the status of Blacks today?

_____

_____

_____

_____

_____

_____

_____

_____

For Further Research

Harriet Tubman was one of the most famous abolitionists connected with the underground railroad. Find out the routes taken by this famous "road to freedom" and the names of other leaders of the movement.

BARBARA WALTERS

Whenever polls are conducted to determine the most admired and influential women in America, the name of Barbara Walters is certain to be somewhere near the top of the list. Her appearances as a cohost on the *Today* show and later as one of the anchors of the *ABC Evening News* made her face and name a household regular throughout America. Her in-depth interviews with some of the most famous and sought-after personalities have become her trademark.

She was born in 1931, in Boston, Massachusetts, the daughter of a Latin Quarter nightclub owner. She grew up in an environment where celebrities and famous people were commonplace, as her father entertained often. After graduating from Sarah Lawrence College, she began to work toward a master's degree in education, but she landed a job as an assistant to the publicity director of WRCA-WRCA TV. She later moved up as women's program producer at WPIX. From there Barbara Walters became a public affairs producer and writer for CBS and was assigned to their early morning show. Her next move was to the competition, NBC, where Dave Garroway hired her as a writer to prepare scripts slanted toward women. She tried several times to get into the limelight of *Today* but was always denied because she wasn't a "recognized" name. Finally, when Maureen O'Sullivan abruptly quit the *Today* show, Barbara got her chance, on a trial basis. She began appearing regularly with program host Hugh Downs and brought interviews to the show no one else was able to obtain. Although she has often been criticized as being uncomfortably probing in her interviews, she feels her strong suit is getting people to open up and say what they have to say by being able to put them at ease.

She left the *Today* show in 1976 to work for ABC as co-anchor of the *ABC Evening News* with Harry Reasoner. Her five-year, $5 million contract made her the highest paid journalist as well as being the first woman to host one of the major network evening news presentations. More recently she has worked on special assignments and done several "Barbara Walters" TV specials for ABC. Although she supports advances toward equality for women, she is a moderate on the issue, preferring the feminine role of being a mother and filling the other traditional roles reserved for women. Barbara Walters currently lives in New York City with her teenage daughter Jacqueline.

Name _____

For Thinking and Discussing

1. How did Barbara Walters' childhood help her later in her career as a newswoman?

    _____

    _____

    _____

    _____

2. How did Barbara Walters get her "break" into big-time television on the *Today* show?

    _____

    _____

    _____

    _____

3. Once she was able to convince NBC executives she belonged on the "right side" of the camera, she became an overnight success with the American public. Why do you think she was so widely accepted even though she didn't have a recognized name?

    _____

    _____

    _____

    _____

4. To what does Barbara Walters consider her secret in getting those she interviews to open up and answer honestly and completely?

    _____

    _____

    _____

    _____

    _____

    _____

Name _____

5. What does Barbara Walters mean when she says she is a "moderate" on the issue of women's liberation?

_____

_____

_____

_____

_____

_____

_____

_____

For Further Research

Barbara Walters has interviewed people from all walks of life, including the rich and the famous and the not-so-rich and the not-so-famous. Find out and list some of those she found most interesting and why she considered them such.

MARTHA WASHINGTON

Though her place in history was established through the fame and efforts of her husband George, Martha Washington distinguished her own mark in time through her undying efforts to add dignity to the new democracy as its first First Lady.

She was born the daughter of a Virginia squire. Though her formal education was limited to what she learned on the plantation, she was well-versed in polite conversation, dancing, and music as well as all the other aspects of social grace that were all a part of the landed gentry. At the age of seventeen she married Colonel Daniel Parke Custis and the couple had four children, two who died in infancy. Custis himself died at an early age, leaving Martha a widow at the age of 25. She had many suitors, but she accepted George Washington's proposal of marriage, and she became totally devoted to him for the rest of her life. The couple had no children but raised the young daughter and son Martha had from her marriage to Custis.

George's involvement in the emerging new nation, took him away from his beloved Martha and Mount Vernon on many occasions, but Martha accepted this and followed her husband whenever she could. When he was leading his troops during the Revolution, she was often near his side, tending to the sick and wounded and providing cheer and comfort during troubled times. When the war was over, she was happy at the thought of spending the rest of their lives together at Mount Vernon. However, this was not to be. The young nation called on George once again, this time to serve as its first President. Less than thrilled at the idea of sharing her husband again, Martha nonetheless set about doing her best to dignify the new nation by bringing grace and charm to her role as First Lady. She not only did what was asked of her, but established precedents that would be followed by others on matters like receiving guests and entertaining.

Martha found New York City society less lively and appealing than Philadelphia, but she met several fine ladies and became especially close to Abigail Adams, wife of the Vice President. She was delighted when Washington announced his retirement after two terms as President, and she joyed at the thought of returning to their stately mansion, Mount Vernon. However, George and Martha had only two more years together as George died in 1799. Martha mourned his passing and died in 1802.

Name _____

For Thinking and Discussing

1. Why didn't Martha Washington receive with enthusiasm her husband's election to the presidency?

_____
_____
_____
_____

2. What did Martha think of New York City as the nation's capital?

_____
_____
_____
_____

3. It is said that Martha complemented the beautiful estate (Mount Vernon) of her husband George. In what way did she contribute to its thriving success and reputation as one of the finest in all the "new land"?

_____
_____
_____
_____

4. How did Martha serve her husband and her country during the Revolution?

_____
_____
_____
_____

Name _____

5. Why was the surrender of Yorktown by Cornwallis (bringing a victorious end to the Revolution) less than a happy moment for both George and Martha?

_____

_____

_____

_____

_____

_____

_____

_____

_____

For Further Research

Martha's devotion to her husband George was born out of the love and respect she had for him as a man. She was very aware of his place in history and wanted that place to be one fondly and well-remembered. What she did not realize was her own mark would be made as well. Cite all the reasons you can that led to Martha Washington's own indelible mark in time.

FRANCES WILLARD

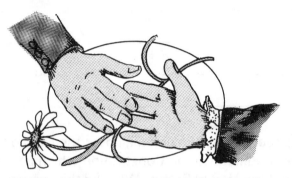

The late 1800's saw women's clubs springing up all over the United States. Although the position of women was far from the equal of men, the mere fact that they were organizing publicly and discussing freely issues of genuine concern was a giant step forward for them. None of these clubs or organizations were as active as Frances Willard's Woman's Christian Temperance Union. Its membership spanned the entire country and boasted of over 200,000 strong.

Frances Willard was one of the most influential women in the United States as she served as the Temperance Union's president from 1879 until her death in 1898. Under her leadership the organization enlisted tens of thousands of women who descended on the saloons of America declaring war on alcohol and the evils accompanied by its use. Men were offended by the tactics used by the W.C.T.U. and often regarded their ambitions as an attack on masculinity itself! The women marched and prayed, and their "military" attack on evil caused insecurity among men.

Perhaps Frances' capacity for organization was her strongest attribute, but she also approached her goals with both tact and persuasion. She knew how to make her programs work and viewed W.C.T.U. as actually more than a temperance movement against alcohol. Now was the opportunity for women to expand their status in other areas of social reform as well.

Her ten years of speaking engagements all over the country inspired women to support her Home Protection program, which covered literally everything from woman suffrage to prison reform. Her political ambitions led her to attempt to unite two powerful reform parties (Prohibition Party and Knights of Labor) into a coalition of close to one million votes. Her attempts failed, however, as a rival who was jealous of her success convinced the Prohibition Party to go their own way. She was a very persuasive and convincing speaker, and even though she often faced a hostile crowd, she had tactful ways of gaining their attention. When she talked she made every new program sound like an absolutely necessary and challenging part of a woman's life, and her very presence brought with it an air of excitement. When Frances Willard died in 1898, her death was mourned by thousands, both women and men, throughout the nation.

Name _____

For Thinking and Discussing

1. What exactly were the goals of the Woman's Christian Temperance Union?

_____
_____
_____
_____

2. The ultimate goal of the W.C.T.U. was prohibition of alcohol all over the United States. Their goal was realized with the 18th Amendment to the Constitution which banned the production and sale of alcohol throughout the United States. Why did this movement fail and eventually lead to the 21st Amendment, which repealed the 18th?

_____
_____
_____
_____

3. Frances Willard's work in reform extended far beyond the prohibition of alcohol. In fact, her Home Protection Program covered several other areas of reform. Find out from another source the "umbrella" of reform she proposed under this plan.

_____
_____
_____
_____

4. Why were many men violently opposed to the very existence of the Women's Christian Temperance Union, when in effect they were actually only attempting to rid the world of the evils that existed?

_____
_____
_____
_____

Name _____

5. What qualities would you think necessary to the personality of Frances Willard to achieve the accomplishments she made?

_____

_____

_____

_____

_____

_____

_____

_____

For Further Research

Find out about the strength of the Woman's Christian Temperance Union, which survives yet today, as well as its goals.

BABE DIDRIKSON ZAHARIAS

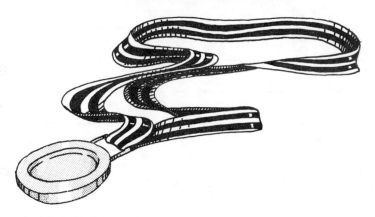

Babe Didrikson was born in Texas, the daughter of Norwegian parents who also had six other children. Although the family was always short on money, the Didriksons were a caring and loving close-knit family. As a girl, Babe was too short to make the high school basketball team. When she was a freshman and sophomore she stood only 5'1''. By her junior year her talents began to shine and she became a star. Her first big team was an AAU team sponsored by Employers Casualty Company of Dallas. Her coach Colonel M. J. McCombs, made certain she got a job with the company to help offset her expenses. It was while working here that she became interested in track and field and she soon became a star. In fact in 1932 she was sent to the National AAU Championships in Chicago as a ''one-girl'' team. She entered eight events, won five, tied for a sixth and accumulated enough points to win the team championship by herself! The 1932 Los Angeles Olympic Games followed, where she won gold medals in the javelin and 80-meter hurdles and a silver medal in the high jump.

Her interest in golf began when the great sports writer Grantland Rice invited her to play golf for the first time. Her athletic achievement got her briefly into show business, but the lure of the great outdoors took her back to golf, where she became a champion, winning the Texas Women's Championship in 1934. Twenty-seven days later she was ruled a professional because she had accepted money from other sports. Because there were few professional tournaments, she tried to make a living doing exhibitions with Gene Sarazen. But she realized that all the good tournaments were for amateurs, so she applied for amateur status once again.

In 1938 she met and later married George Zaharias, a professional wrestler who became her inspiration through golf and life itself. In 1943 she was reinstated as an amateur and immediately began winning tournaments. In fact she won an unheard of seventeen tournaments in a row, including the Women's British Amateur, a tournament never before won by an American. She captured the hearts of fans wherever she went, and her courage in fighting back to the top by winning the U.S. Open just eight months after a major operation for cancer stands as one of the greatest sports stories of all time. However, Babe encountered cancer a second time in 1955, and this time was not able to win the battle, succumbing to the disease in 1956.

Name _____

For Thinking and Discussing

1. What was the incident that caused Babe to be declared a professional golfer, even though she had never accepted money for golf?

_____
_____
_____
_____

2. After the Olympic Games, Babe's name was quite prominent in sports circles everywhere, yet she always had a problem getting enough money to live comfortably. How do you explain this?

_____
_____
_____
_____

3. What is the difference between an amateur and a professional?

_____
_____
_____
_____

4. What steps did Babe have to endure to regain her amateur status?

_____
_____
_____
_____

Name _____

5. Babe, along with her husband George, worked very hard to help initiate the Ladies' Professional Golf Association. What advantage was it to Babe to have an LPGA tour?

_____

_____

_____

_____

_____

_____

_____

_____

For Further Research

In 1949 when the LPGA was formed, the women played for anything they could get. The total prize money for that year was around $15,000. By 1955 they were playing for $200,000. How much do the ladies play for today and how does this compare to the amount of money at stake on the men's professional golf tour?

MY MOST
FAMOUS WOMAN

Name _____

Now that you've finished your study of the forty women highlighted in this book, it's time to make your choice. Your assignment is to reflect back on what you've read and decide the American female you consider the most famous of them all. Support your choice with evidence from your reading as well as discussing your personal reason for the choice you made.

_____

_____

_____

_____

_____

_____

_____

_____

_____

_____

_____

_____

_____

PARTNERS IN PROGRESS

This exciting and challenging game for the entire class provides the perfect finish to your year-long study of our nation's most famous women. The two hundred trivia questions are based on the biographical information, the answers to the questions and the research activities that follow. However, there are some answers to questions that will surface through the general reading and research of other sources and a few others offered as real "challenges." There are five questions on each card for a total of forty game cards included. The correct answer to each corresponding question is found on the back of the card. To ensure the durability of the game cards and to make them easier to handle, it is suggested that they either be laminated or covered with Con-Tact paper before being cut apart. If the teacher wants the children to have advance practice time before playing the game, both sides of each card should be reproduced before the cards are cut apart.

To play the game, the class is divided into as many teams as desired, but three to five players per team usually work best. Order of play is determined by a roll of the die with the team having the highest roll going first. The cards are shuffled and a representative from the first team rolls the die. The top card is chosen, and the teacher reads the numbered question on the card that corresponds to the number of spots showing on the die. If a six is rolled, that player loses his turn. The members of that team then have ten seconds to report their answer. They may confer among themselves, but the first answer heard is the answer that must be used. If the answer is correct, that team is awarded a point. The card used is turned over and the next card is drawn and play advances to the next team. If the answer is incorrect, the next team must answer the missed question.

The first team to score twenty points is declared the winning team. Fewer or more point goals may be used as time allows. A variation is to make questions in later rounds worth more points. If this is done, the winning goal should be adjusted accordingly. A spinner can be used in place of a die if desired. The game also becomes a useful learning tool for two children in a learning center. The same rules apply, but a quiet version involves a generic gameboard, a marker for each player and as many questions as needed to get the winner from *start* to *finish* on the gameboard.

1. She was awarded the 1931 Nobel Peace Prize for her efforts.
2. She was known as Moses to her people.
3. She was once "Today's girl."
4. She gave up the pursuit of a career in voice and piano to marry an Atlanta minister.
5. She was known in Europe simply as "The Pearl."

---

1. She wrote *Little Women*.
2. She began singing in the junior choir of the Baptist Church at the age of six.
3. On June 18, 1983, she became the first American woman to fly in space.
4. She fought for the rights of the people of the tough Bedford-Stuyvesant section of Brooklyn, New York.
5. She spent her youth in such fashionable places as Fifth Avenue, Easthampton, Vassar and George Washington Universities.

---

1. She won a record seventeen amateur golf tournaments in a row.
2. She once set up a clothesline in the East Room of the President's house.
3. *Philadelphia Story* was written especially for her.
4. She published a weekly paper called *The Revolution*.
5. Her long-running television series was called *The French Chef.*

---

1. Veteran acting teacher Lee Strasberg taught her "The Method."
2. The city of New Orleans, her birthplace, was reflected in her singing style.
3. She was at one time the managing editor of *Vanity Fair*.
4. Her autobiography is called *Blackberry Winter*.
5. She was the cofounder of *Ms.* magazine.

---

1. Her first marriage to Daniel Parke Custis ended in tragedy when he died, and she was left widowed at the age of twenty-five.
2. When she spoke in public, her high-pitched voice contained an uncontrollable giggle, which she had to practice hard to overcome.
3. She was born Anna Mary Robertson.
4. She was the first player in women's tennis to win $1 million.
5. She was born Claudia Alta Taylor.

---

1. The story of her disappearance was one of the real mysteries of modern times.
2. Her father was an advocate of the Socratic method of teaching children, and he ran a school in Boston called the Temple School.
3. She was the only woman to ever serve in both houses of Congress.
4. She turned to making cardboard houses with papier-mache when her husband lost all his money.
5. She considered Prohibition the "Hope of Our Country."

---

1. She was the first woman to solo across the Atlantic.
2. She was one of America's most noted anthropologists.
3. On her birth certificate, her name was misspelled with an *a* on the end rather than an *e,* which it should have been.
4. She won a Pulitzer Prize in 1932.
5. The story of her life was entitled *Movin' on Up.*

---

1. She filled the role of Elaine Raleigh, the singing actress in the radio soap opera *Our Gal Sunday.*
2. This Shoshoni Indian guide helped Lewis and Clark explore the territory called Louisiana.
3. She began her political career by representing the tough working class ethnic people of Queens, New York.
4. The great sportswriter Grantland Rice introduced her to the sport that would become her first love.
5. She hosted the nation's first Inaugural Ball.

1. Louisa May Alcott
2. Marian Anderson
3. Sally Ride
4. Shirley Chisholm
5. Jacqueline Kennedy Onassis

1. Jane Addams
2. Harriet Tubman
3. Barbara Walters
4. Coretta King
5. Pearl Buck

1. Jane Fonda
2. Mahalia Jackson
3. Clara Boothe Luce
4. Margaret Mead
5. Gloria Steinem

1. Babe Didrikson Zaharias
2. Abigail Adams
3. Katharine Hepburn
4. Susan B. Anthony
5. Julia Child

1. Amelia Earhart
2. Louisa May Alcott
3. Margaret Chase Smith
4. Emily Post
5. Frances Willard

1. Martha Washington
2. Eleanor Roosevelt
3. Grandma Moses
4. Chris Evert
5. Lady Bird Johnson

1. Beverly Sills
2. Sacagawea
3. Geraldine Ferraro
4. Babe Didrikson Zaharias
5. Dolley Madison

1. Amelia Earhart
2. Margaret Mead
3. Diana Ross
4. Pearl Buck
5. Mahalia Jackson

Card 1
1. She sold her first painting when she was seventy-eight years old.
2. She firmly supported her husband's New Deal.
3. She wrote the book *Mastering the Art of French Cooking* published in 1961.
4. Her life story was portrayed in *The Miracle Worker.*
5. She won a best actress Oscar for her performance in *Klute.*

Card 2
1. She starred in a number of box office hits opposite her good friend Spencer Tracy.
2. She began playing tennis for money on her eighteenth birthday.
3. She served as a United States Ambassador to Italy between 1953 and 1957.
4. She met her husband John in law school at Stanford, where he was also a student.
5. In 1972 she launched a serious campaign to become President, but she didn't get enough votes in the primaries to have her name placed on the ballot.

Card 3
1. She gave several "freedom concerts" to illustrate the history of the Civil Rights movement.
2. She often entertained by having lobster flown in from her home state.
3. She was once ranked eighteenth nationally among junior tennis players.
4. Her Aunt Effie Patillo helped to raise her when her mother died.
5. She served as hostess in the White House longer than anyone else—sixteen years.

Card 4
1. During the Revolutionary War, she tended the sick and wounded and offered them comfort and cheer.
2. Her stoic, almost Spartan, behavior during the aftermath of her husband's assassination was admired by the entire world.
3. She won gold medals in the javelin and 80-meter hurdles in the 1932 Olympics.
4. Her less famous husband was Toussaint Charbonneau, a French-Canadian trader.
5. Her name has come to mean good manners.

Card 5
1. She is the most persuasive spokesperson for the feminist movement in America.
2. She was the first woman doctor in the United States.
3. The main themes she emphasized throughout her speeches were home and family.
4. She was the first President's wife to live in the new capital of Washington, D.C.
5. Her autobiography is entitled *Bubbles: A Self-Portrait.*

Card 6
1. She wrote *Uncle Tom's Cabin.*
2. She was the first woman to host a major network evening news show.
3. She carried an accent which reflected her British elementary school education and her West Indian origin.
4. As a child she roamed the fields with Henry David Thoreau.
5. Most of her roles recently have dealt with social messages.

Card 7
1. In 1938 she was awarded the Nobel Prize for Literature.
2. At birth her name contained three *a*'s, but she later dropped one.
3. She was the first woman ever awarded the distinguished Flying Cross.
4. She was the first woman to run for Vice President as a major party candidate.
5. She closed many of her concerts with John Payne's "Crucifixion."

Card 8
1. It is said that her book helped to start the Civil War.
2. She established a cooking school, L'Ecole des Trois Gourmandes, with two French women.
3. Her work began on Halstead Street in Chicago, Illinois.
4. She was called "Cinderella in sneakers" by members of the press.
5. She was a "wanted" woman, with rewards for her capture totalling $40,000.

1. Katharine Hepburn
2. Chris Evert
3. Clara Boothe Luce
4. Sandra Day O'Connor
5. Shirley Chisholm

1. Grandma Moses
2. Eleanor Roosevelt
3. Julia Child
4. Helen Keller
5. Jane Fonda

1. Martha Washington
2. Jacqueline Kennedy Onassis
3. Babe Didrikson Zaharias
4. Sacagawea
5. Emily Post

1. Coretta King
2. Margaret Chase Smith
3. Sally Ride
4. Lady Bird Johnson
5. Dolley Madison

1. Harriet Beecher Stowe
2. Barbara Walters
3. Shirley Chisholm
4. Louisa May Alcott
5. Jane Fonda

1. Gloria Steinem
2. Elizabeth Blackwell
3. Frances Willard
4. Abigail Adams
5. Beverly Sills

1. Harriet Beecher Stowe
2. Julia Child
3. Jane Addams
4. Chris Evert
5. Harriet Tubman

1. Pearl Buck
2. Barbra Streisand
3. Amelia Earhart
4. Geraldine Ferraro
5. Marian Anderson

1. She was chosen by Navy Captain Robert L. Crippen as "the best person for the job."
2. She served the longest time ever as First Lady.
3. Her place in history was earned through her unselfish dedication to social reform and the settlement house.
4. She had the word *obey* stricken from her marriage vows.
5. She played the role of blues singer Billie Holiday in the movie *Lady Sings the Blues*.

---

1. She was arrested and fined $100 in 1872 for voting in a presidential election, but she never paid the fine.
2. Her husband called her Patsy.
3. She is married to former activist and present California legislator Tom Hayden.
4. She was the first woman to deliver a keynote speech at a national convention during prime time coverage by the news media.
5. She carried her son on her back during a famous historical trek.

---

1. A United States postage stamp was issued in her honor in 1978.
2. The ugliness of the male-dominated marriage her mother suffered caused her to fight for women's rights when she grew older.
3. *The Good Earth* was her most famous work.
4. Her personal symbol was a rose, which she wore daily as an accessory to her dress.
5. Because of a cast in one eye, she felt she would never appeal to a man, so she devoted her life to advancing the rights of women.

---

1. The $1 million a year she received with ABC made her the highest paid journalist ever.
2. She is the only actress to have been nominated four times for the best actress Academy Award.
3. She rescued many national treasures just before the British burned the Palace during the War of 1812.
4. She helped to promote the "Black Is Beautiful" campaign.
5. Because of her handicap, she developed a highly sensitive awareness of her surroundings.

---

1. At the age of twenty-seven, she became the only person ever to have won all of the major awards in the entertainment industry.
2. The March family in her books was in reality her own family.
3. She had to overcome a problem of speaking before large groups of people when her pulse quickened, her mouth became dry, and her teeth would often chatter.
4. Her life was threatened when she bought her first home in a white neighborhood in Chicago.
5. When her husband died, she redirected her focus in life by serving as the United States delegate to the United Nations.

---

1. As a child, her mind wandered beyond her academic subjects to the music room.
2. Her causes were women's rights and antislavery; her weapons were her eloquent persuasive speaking voice and even temper.
3. She considered the three great evils of life racism, poverty, and war.
4. She considered interior decorating her true calling, even though it is not what made her famous.
5. She was a firm believer in equal rights for women, but she refused to march in her graduation because she considered it unladylike.

---

1. She made her mark in history as one of America's most famous hostesses to foreign leaders and diplomats.
2. Her interest in humankind led her to accept a position as curator at the Museum of Natural History.
3. Her career in politics began with an appointment to fill a vacancy in the Arizona State Senate.
4. Her first book was entitled *Outrageous Acts and Everyday Rebellions*.
5. It was said of her by Toscanini: "A voice like hers comes once in a century!"

---

1. Her devotion to medicine gave her the strength to deal with those who scorned and ridiculed her work.
2. She parlayed her less than gorgeous looks into an offbeat image copied by others.
3. As a freshman in Congress, her work was admired by House Speaker Tip O'Neill, who helped her get on important committees.
4. Her last published book was entitled *Culture and Commitment*.
5. She was married to one President and the mother of another.

127

1. Susan B. Anthony
2. Martha Washington
3. Jane Fonda
4. Clara Boothe Luce
5. Sacagawea

1. Sally Ride
2. Eleanor Roosevelt
3. Jane Addams
4. Lucy Stone
5. Diana Ross

1. Barbara Walters
2. Katharine Hepburn
3. Dolley Madison
4. Diana Ross
5. Helen Keller

1. Harriet Tubman
2. Lucy Stone
3. Pearl Buck
4. Margaret Chase Smith
5. Susan B. Anthony

1. Marian Anderson
2. Lucy Stone
3. Coretta King
4. Emily Post
5. Elizabeth Blackwell

1. Barbra Streisand
2. Louisa May Alcott
3. Gloria Steinem
4. Mahalia Jackson
5. Eleanor Roosevelt

1. Elizabeth Blackwell
2. Barbra Streisand
3. Geraldine Ferraro
4. Margaret Mead
5. Abigail Adams

1. Jacqueline Kennedy Onassis
2. Margaret Mead
3. Sandra Day O'Connor
4. Gloria Steinem
5. Marian Anderson

Box 1

1. She championed fair play for the poor and helped thousands of United States immigrants.
2. Her daughter Luci was the first daughter of a President to marry while her father was in office since 1914.
3. In 1979 she became the first woman to have her picture on a coin in general circulation.
4. Her name literally means "bird woman."
5. She was the director of the Friends Day Nursery and later became a noted authority on early childhood education.

Box 2

1. She personally led nineteen rescue missions to free Blacks from slavery.
2. Her exposure to European culture and tradition (while she was with her husband there) accounted for her unpopularity as First Lady.
3. She turned a $31,000 investment in a radio station and VHF TV channel into a $5 million windfall.
4. Her first New York stage appearance was in *Night Hostess* under the name of Katharine Burns.
5. She started a clinic in a New York City slum because her attempt at a private practice was not successful.

Box 3

1. She once wrote that her life in the sanitarium had been ". . . among her most pleasant moments ever . . . ."
2. She became Ronald Reagan's "person for all seasons."
3. Her most famous novels used China as their setting.
4. She was appointed United States Ambassador to Brazil but resigned before assuming the position.
5. Her first published book was a novel entitled *The Flight of the Moth.*

Box 4

1. She has appeared several times with the national symphony as narrator of Aaron Copland's *A Lincoln Portrait.*
2. She has a "Boston accent with a New York overlay" but was welcomed into millions of homes every evening at five thirty.
3. She graduated from the world's largest high school with straight A's.
4. Her home was an estate called Montpelier.
5. She was the first divorcee to use her maiden name with that of her husband.

Box 5

1. She advocated a thirty-nine-point social reform that would advance the cause of women called the Home Protection Program.
2. She was the aviation editor of *Cosmopolitan* magazine.
3. She refused to accept the name of her husband Henry Blackwell when the couple married.
4. Her highly successful autobiography was entitled *The Story of My Life.*
5. The 19th Amendment to the U.S. Constitution bears her name.

Box 6

1. Her book was by far the most popular of the nineteenth century selling over 500,000 copies and being translated into over twenty foreign languages.
2. Her role as First Lady was enhanced by her being a part of the landed gentry.
3. Her best-known book was called *Coming of Age in Samoa.*
4. She grew up in Concord, Massachusetts, surrounded by literary giants.
5. In 1932 at the age of three, she won first prize in the "Miss Beautiful Baby" contest.

Box 7

1. Her paintings reflected the moods and thoughts of her rural world.
2. Her husband Paul was a gastronome.
3. Her youthful appearance, winning personality, and all-American system of values made her Miss America Pie.
4. She runs four to five miles a day, works out with weights, and has become acclimated to increased g force.
5. She was the founder of the New York Infirmary for Women and Children.

Box 8

1. Her autobiography is entitled *Declaration of Conscience.*
2. She sang "The Star-Spangled Banner" at John F. Kennedy's Inauguration.
3. She once gave a concert attended by over 75,000 people at the Lincoln Memorial in Washington, D.C.
4. When entertaining, she often provided her guests with historic or extravagant backgrounds to add to the impression of the moment.
5. She chaired the 1984 Democratic Platform committee.

1. Harriet Tubman
2. Abigail Adams
3. Lady Bird Johnson
4. Katharine Hepburn
5. Elizabeth Blackwell

1. Jane Addams
2. Lady Bird Johnson
3. Susan B. Anthony
4. Sacagawea
5. Shirley Chisholm

1. Coretta King
2. Barbara Walters
3. Barbra Streisand
4. Dolley Madison
5. Emily Post

1. Harriet Beecher Stowe
2. Sandra Day O'Connor
3. Pearl Buck
4. Clara Boothe Luce
5. Emily Post

1. Harriet Beecher Stowe
2. Martha Washington
3. Margaret Mead
4. Louisa May Alcott
5. Beverly Sills

1. Frances Willard
2. Amelia Earhart
3. Lucy Stone
4. Helen Keller
5. Susan B. Anthony

1. Margaret Chase Smith
2. Mahalia Jackson
3. Marian Anderson
4. Jacqueline Kennedy Onassis
5. Geraldine Ferraro

1. Grandma Moses
2. Julia Child
3. Chris Evert
4. Sally Ride
5. Elizabeth Blackwell

Box 1:

1. Many historians agree with Harry Truman's statement "She would have made a better President than her husband."
2. She was idolized by thousands for her bravado in the sky.
3. She was an author and playwright—perhaps her most successful play being *The Women*.
4. She wrote a syndicated newspaper column titled, "My Day."
5. She won the role of Cleopatra in *Julius Caesar*.

Box 2:

1. Her ability on a clay surface made her unbeatable.
2. She was the first black woman to serve in Congress.
3. Her exercise and health salons were called "Workout."
4. Her career really began when she landed a job writing scripts for the *CBS Morning News*.
5. She was the *Funny Girl.*

Box 3:

1. She was called the "Joan of Ark" of the Republican Party.
2. She was once a *Playboy* bunny.
3. Her husband was so dictatorial that she was temporarily traumatized into paralysis.
4. She was born Araminta Ross.
5. She was the first First Lady.

Box 4:

1. She was once part of a singing group called the Primettes.
2. She was married to Isaac Hockenhull, but the marriage ended in divorce.
3. She was raised in a family of ten children, and she had ten children of her own.
4. She flew in the *Challenger*.
5. She was the first American woman explorer.

Box 5:

1. Years after her husband was slain by an assassin's bullet, she married a wealthy Greek tycoon.
2. Her "beautification" program took her over 200,000 miles.
3. She was the prim and proper missionary opposite Humphrey Bogart in *The African Queen.*
4. She ran a race with Walter Mondale in 1984.
5. The kitchen was her favorite room.

Box 6:

1. She was born Belle Miriam Silverman.
2. Her first exhibition was called "What a Farmwife Painted."
3. She is the first woman to become a member of the U.S. Supreme Court.
4. Her less famous name was one time Dorothy Payne Todd.
5. She was called a "black Madonna" by the press.

Box 7:

1. Her teacher was Anne Sullivan.
2. For God, for Home, and Native Land was her motto and that of the W.C.T.U.
3. Her work was called a "Cathedral of Humanity."
4. She married a professional wrestler.
5. She was the first woman from Massachusetts to earn a college degree.

Box 8:

1. She grew up on a 155,000-acre ranch called the Lazy B Ranch.
2. Her voice was part of the "Motown Sound."
3. "I've always had the urge to do things better than anyone else."
4. She was President of the W.C.T.U. for almost twenty years.
5. She wrote the book *Out of the Dark.*

1. Chris Evert
2. Shirley Chisholm
3. Jane Fonda
4. Barbara Walters
5. Barbra Streisand

1. Abigail Adams
2. Amelia Earhart
3. Clara Boothe Luce
4. Eleanor Roosevelt
5. Beverly Sills

1. Diana Ross
2. Mahalia Jackson
3. Grandma Moses
4. Sally Ride
5. Sacagawea

1. Margaret Chase Smith
2. Gloria Steinem
3. Harriet Beecher Stowe
4. Harriet Tubman
5. Martha Washington

1. Beverly Sills
2. Grandma Moses
3. Sandra Day O'Connor
4. Dolley Madison
5. Coretta King

1. Jacqueline Kennedy Onassis
2. Lady Bird Johnson
3. Katharine Hepburn
4. Geraldine Ferraro
5. Julia Child

1. Sandra Day O'Connor
2. Diana Ross
3. Babe Didrickson Zaharias
4. Frances Willard
5. Helen Keller

1. Helen Keller
2. Frances Willard
3. Jane Addams
4. Babe Didrikson Zaharias
5. Lucy Stone

BIBLIOGRAPHY

Akers, Charles W. *Abigail Adams: An American Woman*, Little, Brown, 1980.
Kelly, Regina Z. *Abigail Adams*, Houghton Mifflin, 1962.
Peterson, Helen, *Abigail Adams: Dear Partner*, Garrard, 1967.

Johnson, Ann Donegan, *The Value of Friendship: The Story of Jane Addams*, Value Communications, 1978.
Judson, Clara, *City Neighbors: The Story of Jane Addams*, Scribner, 1951.
Keller, Gail, *Jane Addams*, Crowell, 1971.
Wise, Winifred E., *Jane Addams of Hull House*, Harcourt, 1935.

Colver, Anne, *Louisa May Alcott: Author of Little Women*, Garrard, 1969.
Fisher, Aileen, and Rabe, Oliver, *We Alcotts*, Atheneum, 1968.
Meigs, Cornelia, *Invincible Louisa*, Little, 1933.
Papashvily, Helen, *Louisa May Alcott*, Houghton Mifflin, 1965.

Anderson, Marian, *My Lord, What a Morning*, Viking, 1956, Avon, 1964.
Newman, Shirlee, *Marian Anderson: Lady from Philadelphia*, Westminster, 1966.
Tobias, Tobi, *Marian Anderson*, Crowell, 1972.

Grant, Matthew G., *Susan B. Anthony*, Creative Education/Children's Press, 1974.
Noble, Iris, *Susan B. Anthony*, Messner, 1975.
Peterson, Helen S., *Susan B. Anthony: Pioneer in Women's Rights*, Garrard, 1971.
Salsini, Barbara, *Susan B. Anthony: A Crusader for Women's Rights*, SamHar Press, 1972.

Clapp, Patricia, *Dr. Elizabeth: A Biography of the First Woman Doctor*, Lothrop, 1974.
Matthew, Scott, *The First Woman of Medicine: The Story of Elizabeth Blackwell*, Contemporary Perspectives, 1978.
Wilson, Dorothy Clarke, *Lone Woman: The Story of Elizabeth Blackwell*, Little, 1970.

Block, Irvin, *The Lives of Pearl Buck: A Tale of China and America*, Crowell, 1973.
Buck, Pearl S., *My Several Worlds: A Personal Record,* Day, 1954.
Schoen, Celin V., *Pearl Buck: Famed American Author of Oriental Stories*, SamHar Press, 1972.
Westervelt, Virginia, *Pearl Buck: A Biographical Novel*, Nelson, 1979.

Life, October 21, 1966.
Newsweek, July 15, 1963.
Saturday Evening Post, August 8, 1964.
Time, March 20, 1964 and November 25, 1966.

Brownmiller, Susan, *Shirley Chisholm*, Archway, 1970.
Chisholm, Shirley, *Unbought and Unbossed*, Houghton Mifflin, 1970.
Haskins, James, *Fighting Shirley Chisholm*, Dial, 1975.
Hicks, Nancy, *The Honorable Shirley Chisholm: Congresswoman from Brooklyn*, Lion, 1971.

Davis, Burke, *Amelia Earhart*, Putnam, 1972.
Earhart, Amelia, *Last Flight*, Harcourt, 1938 (reprint of 1937 edition).
Howe, Jane Moore, *Amelia Earhart: Kansas Girl*, Bobbs-Merrill, 1950.
Mann, Peggy, *Amelia Earhart: First Lady of Flight*, Coward, 1970.

Burchard, S.H., *Chris Evert,* Harcourt, 1976.
Phillips, Betty Lou, *Chris Evert: First Lady of Tennis*, Messner, 1977.
Sabin, Francene, *Set Point: The Story of Chris Evert*, Putnam, 1977.
Schmitz, Dorothy Childers, *Chris Evert: Women's Tennis Champion*, Crestwood, 1977.

Fox, Mary Virginia, and Weston, Paul, *Jane Fonda: Something to Fight For*, Dillon, 1980.

Life, January 5, 1968.
New York Times, April 27, 1969.
Washington (D.C.) Post, September 1, 1969.

Cornell, Jean Gay, *Mahalia Jackson: Queen of Gospel Song,* Garrard, 1974.
Dunham, Montrew, *Mahalia Jackson: Young Gospel Singer*, Bobbs-Merrill, 1974.
Jackson, Jesse, *Make a Joyful Noise unto the Lord: The Life of Mahalia Jackson, Queen of Gospel Singers*, Crowell, 1974.
McDearmon, Kay, *Mahalia: Gospel Singer*, Dodd, 1976.

Hickok, Lorena A., *The Story of Helen Keller,* Grosset, 1958.
Keller, Helen, *Story of My Life*, Doubleday, 1954.
Peare, Catherine O., *The Helen Keller Story*, Crowell, 1959.
Tibble, J.W., and Tibble, Anne, *Helen Keller*, Putnam, 1958.

Ebony, September 1968.
Patterson, Lillie, *Coretta Scott King*, Garrard, 1977.
Taylor, Paula, *Coretta Scott King*, Creative Educ. Soc., 1975.

Desmond, Alice Curtis, *Glamourous Dolley Madison*, Dodd, 1946.
Melick, Arden Davis, *Dolley Madison, First Lady*, Putnam, 1970.
Nolan, Jeannette, *Dolley Madison*, Messner, 1959.
Thane, Elswyth, *Dolley Madison: Her Life and Times*, Macmillan, 1970.

Church, Carol Bauer, *Margaret Mead, Student of the Global Village*, Greenhaven Press, 1976.
Frevert, Patricia, *Margaret Mead: Herself*, Creative Education, 1981.
Ludle, Jacqueline, *Margaret Mead*, Watts, 1983.
Mead, Margaret, *Blackberry Winter: My Earlier Years*, Morrow, 1972.
Rice, Edward, *Margaret Mead: A Portrait*, Harper & Row, 1979.

Armstrong, William, *Barefoot in the Grass: The Story of Grandma Moses*, Doubleday, 1970.
Graves, Charles, *Grandma Moses: Favorite Painter*, Garrard, 1969.
Laing, Martha, *Grandma Moses: The Grand Old Lady of American Art*, SamHar Press, 1972.

Greene, Carol, *Sandra Day O'Connor: First Woman on the Supreme Court*, Children's Press, 1982.

O'Connor, Karen, *Sally Ride and the New Astronauts: Scientists in Space*, Watts, 1983.

Davidson, Margaret, *Story of Eleanor Roosevelt*, Four Winds, 1969.
Goodsell, Jane, *Eleanor Roosevelt*, Crowell, 1970.
Graves, Charles, *Eleanor Roosevelt: First Lady of the Land*, Garrard, 1965.

Roosevelt, Eleanor, *The Autobiography of Eleanor Roosevelt*, Harper, 1961.

Haskins, James, *I'm Gonna Make You Love Me*, Dial, 1980.
Life, December 8, 1972.
Time, March 4, 1966 and August 17, 1970.

Burt, Olive, *Sacajawea*, Watts, 1978.
Farnsworth, Frances, *Winged Moccasins: The Story of Sacajawea*, Messner, 1954.
Johnson, Ann Donegan, *The Value of Adventure: The Story of Sacagawea*, Value Communications, 1980.
Skold, Betty Westrom, *Sacagawea*, Dillon, 1977.

Sills, Beverly, *Bubbles: A Self-Portrait*, Grosset, 1976.
Sills, Beverly, *Bubbles: An Encore*, Grosset, 1981.

Fleming, Alice, *Senator from Maine: Margaret Chase Smith*, Crowell, 1969.

Blackwell, Alice Stone, *Lucy Stone: Pioneer of Woman's Rights*, Little, 1930.
Stapelton, Jean, *Vanguard Suffragist: Lucy Stone*, Women's Heritage Series, 1971.

Hooker, Gloria, *I Shall Not Live in Vain*, Concordia, 1978.
Johnson, Johanna, *Harriet and the Runaway Book: The Story of Harriet Beecher Stowe and Uncle Tom's Cabin*, Harper, 1977.
Rouverol, Jean, *Harriet Beecher Stowe: Woman Crusader*, Putnam, 1968.
Scott, John Anthony, *Woman Against Slavery: The Story of Harriet Beecher Stowe*, Crowell, 1978.

Conrad, Earl, *Harriet Tubman: Negro Soldier and Abolitionist*, Troll, 1982.
Heidish, Marcy, *A Woman Called Moses*, Houghton Mifflin, 1976.
Sterling, Dorothy, *Freedom Train*, Doubleday, 1954
Winders, Gertrude, *Harriet Tubman: Freedom Girl*, Bobbs-Merrill, 1969.

Fox, Mary Virginia, and Weston, Paul, *Barbara Walter: The News Her Way*, Dillon, 1980.

Mason, Miriam E., *Frances Willard: Girl Crusader*, Bobbs-Merrill, 1961.

De Grummond, Lena Y., and Delaune, Lynn D., *Babe Didrikson: Girl Athlete*, Bobbs-Merrill, 1963.
Hahn, James, and Hahn, Lynn, *Zaharias!*, Crestwood, 1981.
Smith, Beatrice S., *The Babe: Mildred Didrikson Zaharias*, Raintree, 1976.
Zaharias, Babe Didrikson, *This Life I've Led: An Autobiography*, Barnes, 1955.

ANSWER KEY

ABIGAIL ADAMS

1. While it was good for him to be so concerned about the rights and well-being of other nations, he would do well to be kind to women as well. She was a forerunner of women's rights.
2. He followed in the footsteps of George Washington, who had been a very popular President. He was also concerned with domestic squabbles at home between those who supported the British and those who supported the French, who were warring with each other at the time.
3. She had been exposed to the convention and tradition of European culture, and many in the United States felt her silk and velvety dress and upperclass mannerisms were "too thronelike." She also did not entertain very much.
4. She was exposed to the customs and traditions, the matters of dress and actions of cultured society in Europe. She learned how important grace and charm were to fulfilling such a role.
5. She corresponded with him in much the same manner as she had her husband. Her views on politics and stimulating letters were a major influence in molding him into the making of a President.

JANE ADDAMS

1. She was able to buy the Halstead Street mansion, which she turned into Hull House. She was also able to buy the necessary furnishings and supplies that would keep it going and ensure its success. Her wealth also meant she could devote full time to her work and did not have to get another job.
2. She taught reading, sewing skills and arts and crafts. There was an interest in music with an orchestra and even a "little theater." In short, nothing was ruled out at Hull House. Any concern of any of the members of Hull House was a concern of all. There was a sharing of problems. There was even a kindergarten and a recreation room.
3. She probed into the real causes of poverty and attempted to deal with them on her own terms. She also believed in using trained social workers, and finally, she believed in placing considerable pressure on lawmakers who could bring about reform.
4. She was interested in seeking peace among nations and her ideas were not considered patriotic enough for these groups.
5. She never became loyal to any political party, and she was reluctant to align herself with any special group. While she championed the underdog, her motives were sometimes misunderstood, and she often found herself without support. But that did not keep her from her dogged pursuit of her goals.

LOUISA MAY ALCOTT

1. The March family, which she highlights in the book, is actually the story of her own childhood and experiences of the Alcott family.
2. He felt that the potential of children could best be unlocked through carefully devised questions. Children must know themselves first; and cramming, corporal punishment and strict regimen of the mind (which were the order of the day) had no place in education. His school failed.
3. She not only listened to the conversations they had with her father, but she browsed through their personal libraries and had access to their very thoughts.
4. She volunteered her services as a nurse during the Civil War, and she also firmly supported women's voting rights and the temperance movement.
5. He was a recognized educator of the times plus he had a close personal association with the likes of Emerson, Thoreau, and Holmes. In addition, Bronson always encouraged his daughters to write down their thoughts, and he provided them with stimulating thoughts.

MARIAN ANDERSON

1. She was acutely aware of the rhythm and music of many things one wouldn't normally associate with music. Perhaps it was this sensation and constant awareness that helped to push her toward a career in music.
2. Her return to New York City was a proud moment for her as she had been earlier denied opportunity in the United States because of her race. She wanted to return with a concert that would make them all proud she was an American, and she no doubt felt a handicap would detract from that appearance.
3. She had always loved music. When she became exposed to the talents of famous tenor, Roland Hayes, and she sang with him and saw how he was accepted by the public, she decided it was how she wanted to make a living.
4. She not only loved the music of her race, but she felt like she was a symbol of what they were. She wanted to glorify music that was truly theirs.
5. Although she tried to stay away from the controversies of her race, she was originally scheduled to perform at Constitution Hall. She was denied presumably because of her race and the newspapers aroused public concern. Thus the Lincoln Memorial was an appropriate substitute—to sing near the memorial to the man who had freed her people.

SUSAN B. ANTHONY

1. She fought for better working conditions for women, for women to organize into unions. Her real campaigns were against alcohol and attempting to gain the right to vote for women.
2. His manner of speaking was entertaining, and he was able to gain the attention of crowds under hostile environs, thus allowing the women the opportunity to be heard. He also helped finance the group.
3. They were facing a traditional view that had existed for centuries that a woman's place was in the home.
4. There was constant bickering and disagreement among the top leaders in the movement for women's equality. In fact they eventually separated into two separate camps even though many of their goals were the same.
5. Answers will vary but the general theme should be that she would consider it a setback but not a defeat and would no doubt carry on the fight in the same spirit in which she fought for suffrage.

ELIZABETH BLACKWELL

1. Whenever she was put down, she viewed the situation as one more reason to become a doctor.
2. She was going against the already stereotype of what was "right" for women, i.e., a woman's place is in the home. Professional women were frowned upon.
3. She was unsuccessful in trying to establish herself in areas where medical help was close by. She also felt there was a need to provide medical aid for these people.
4. Her determination to improve the status of women was no doubt spurred on by much of the prejudice and ostracism she faced.
5. Answers will vary, but may include that she was too busy and involved with her own career in medicine to have time for marriage and a family.

PEARL BUCK

1. Her missionary parents raised her in China, and her exposure to the language, customs and traditions in China provided her the background she needed to write about China.
2. She read all the available Chinese novels she could as well as the Chinese classics. Her knowledge of the thousands of characters necessary for the Chinese language served her well once she started writing.
3. Her first education in China came from her mother. She was also taught by an old Chinese nurse. She later enrolled in Randolph-Macon College in the United States. She also studied in Europe before going back to China, where she taught at Nanking University.
4. She already had a name from earlier novels. The book was also her best; and it sold to a book club, which earned its success and instant recognition in the literary world.
5. She was awarded the 1938 Nobel Prize for Literature.

JULIA CHILD

1. While a student at Smith College, they changed the rules of basketball so that they no longer jumped center after each basketball. This offset her height advantage and discouraged her from a career in basketball.
2. Her husband was a gastronome, and Julia was determined to become a good cook, so she took lessons. Then when he was stationed in Paris she was introduced to Simone Beck and Louisette Bertolle and her career was on its way.
3. The success of her book *Mastering the Art of French Cooking* led to media exposure and talk show appearances. On one such occasion, she was preparing an omelette and the response was popular among viewers. Hence the TV series was launched.
4. There are certain techniques that apply to many dishes which must be mastered first. It is also impossible to get good results if time-consuming steps are eliminated or costly ingredients are substituted.
5. Her casual appearance, using only a basic "plan" for the show without a script, and not editing out the errors all added to the show's credibility and helped her pick up fans she might not otherwise have had.

SHIRLEY CHISHOLM

1. When she was only three years old, her parents sent her to Barbados to live for a time with her grandmother. She was a very strict lady and taught Shirley constantly the virtues of pride, courage, and faith.
2. While in college, she was very successful in debates and was encouraged by her professors to enter politics. She tried the education profession, but found her interests in politics and social change too tempting to pass by.
3. She was a very outspoken lady, and she had a mind of her own that did not bow to political pressure and patronage.
4. She (as Susan B. Anthony) was untiringly dedicated to her causes and was made to believe she was also urging women to move into politics, which was also a goal of Susan B. Anthony.
5. She felt President Reagan was unresponsive to the needs of others and that she was working for a hopeless cause.

AMELIA EARHART

1. She encouraged them at every stage of the way.
2. We all need heroes and heroines whom we can admire who have dared and reached out beyond so that others may be encouraged to do the same.
3. She was attempting to fly around the world. On the longest leg of the trip (from New Guinea to Howland Island) she disappeared and was never heard from again.
4. Answers will vary, but she would no doubt be even more of a hero figure than she is now.
5. Although hostilities existed, the U.S. was not in a state of war with Japan and would have no legitimate reason to be surveying their air fields.

CHRIS EVERT

1. Her father was a tennis instructor and her two brothers and two sisters also helped make the Everts a tennis family. Neither parent pushed their children into tennis, but their influence no doubt headed them in that direction.
2. Her two-handed backhand stroke allows her to remain at the baseline and belt drives deep into the opponent's court. She also learned to wait and patiently outlast most of her opponents.
3. The United States Open, Wimbledon, the French Open and the Australian Open
4. She never refused her fans nor the press. She was also attractive to men and popular with teens because of her success in youth. Finally mothers all over the land admired the personal standards she set for herself.
5. Both Jimmy Connors and Chris Evert had personal goals to be the "best" in tennis. To be number one requires a great deal of personal sacrifice, and both chose to pursue their careers in tennis in preference to marriage.

GERALDINE FERRARO

1. She kept her maiden name professionally out of devotion to her mother.
2. Through her concern for the welfare of the victim she dealt with during her job with the Special Victims Bureau
3. She was against mandatory bussing, for a strong defense and backed spending on some of Reagan's nuclear proposals, all this in conflict with the Democratic Party.
4. First, he was fighting an uphill battle and was looking for something that would help him pull off an upset of Reagan. He felt it might be time for a woman and Ferraro was well-qualified. She was also Roman Catholic and had an Italian background, both of which he hoped would draw him votes.
5. She was said to be firm but not abrasive, and she did not alienate nor threaten her male colleagues. She was also close to the Democratic leadership, and the men in the House respected her views.

JANE FONDA

1. As a child she didn't seem to care much about acting. But she was nonetheless very aware of the glamour and material comforts that accompany success in motion pictures. She also was determined to make a name for herself.
2. Strasberg's "Method" was an approach to acting which encouraged actors to experience the roles they played rather than imitate. The idea was to present a more realistic portrayal of the character.
3. Her popularity as an actress placed her in a position of influence among American women. Her attractive figure and healthy appearance no doubt also been in part responsible for the success of her book and videotape on fitness.
4. She feels movie stars have influence over many people and are thus in a position to help bring about social change.
5. She has been answering the bell most of her life, sorting and picking and choosing to follow what was right for her even though it might have led to controversy and unpopularity.

KATHARINE HEPBURN

1. She grew up in an environment where hard work and self-discipline were the order of the day. Her family also refused to accept self-pity by any members of the family.
2. She received an aristocratic Eastern education from private tutors and private schools. At Bryn Mawr College she wanted to become a doctor, but her grades in chemistry were poor and there were few women doctors. So she turned to the drama department and found her niche.
3. After a success on Broadway in *The Warrior's Husband*, she signed with RKO pictures. Her first film, *Bill of Divorcement*, was later followed by the highly acclaimed *Morning Glory* for which she received an Academy Award nomination.
4. The woman is sharp, the man slow. The woman needles him until he shows his authority as he is the ultimate boss—but he must constantly protect his role.
5. She meant that people *must* make changes in this society and that they must face up to the responsibilities and consequences of the choices they make.

MAHALIA JACKSON

1. The early influence of the city where music filled the streets helped to establish her singing style—even though she sang mostly religious music. It was as though the style was etched into her very soul and her voice thrilled audiences everywhere.
2. She'd heard stories about how much better Blacks were treated and how there was much less prejudice and greater chance for a better life. Chicago seemed to offer them the best chance.
3. DuBois listened to her sing spirituals and told her her style was all wrong and that she was a discredit to black singers because white people wouldn't be able to understand them. She was offended and never went back.
4. Ike didn't approve of her travel and he felt she could do much better in a singing career as a blues singer. So he constantly criticized; she likewise was unhappy with her husband's gambling habits.
5. She did not want to sing before those who might laugh at her, and she refused to be a party to helping promote the sale of alcohol (nightclub appearances). She also felt that gospel music was straight from the heart—and singing praises of the Lord's good tidings was what singing was all about.

LADY BIRD JOHNSON

1. When she was two years old, her black nursemaid said she was "as purty as a Lady Bird." Her father liked the comment and began calling her that himself. Others followed.
2. Lyndon had courted Lady Bird only two months when he asked her to marry. She turned him down at first, but when Johnson convinced her father of his worth, Taylor made the statement to his daughter and she changed her mind.
3. She borrowed $10,000 from her father against her inheritance to finance her husband's bid for Congress. Then in 1964 she helped him in his campaign and had already gained the nation's attention and respect the way she performed as First Lady when she was thrust into the position when Kennedy was assassinated and her husband took over as President.
4. Even though she came from a family of wealth, she made good use of her money. Financing her husband's campaign for Congress in the long run was a good investment. Also, her buying the radio and TV stations was a real bonanza financially.
5. Answers will vary, but she would no doubt be in favor of women achieving equality. However, her statement and her personality suggest she would be an activist in the movement.

HELEN KELLER

Questions are value-based and do not require an answer key.

CORETTA KING

1. When she had to walk five miles to school in Herberger, Alabama, each day, she was passed by the school bus carrying white children. She was determined to work for an end to such practices.
2. She met Dr. Martin Luther King, Jr. The couple had similar goals and values about life, so they got married and she began raising a family.
3. Her family was threatened with violence constantly, and she accompanied her husband to rallies and demonstrations whenever possible. Her family was suddenly thrust into the public eye and exposed to many dangers.
4. Both showed remarkable control and courage and remained grief stricken in a dignified manner that was observed by an entire nation.
5. She was a nonviolent person and did not seek revenge, but she did think that Ray had not acted alone in the slaying and that there had been a conspiracy to kill him.

CLARA BOOTHE LUCE

1. Her husband Henry Luce had supported Wilkie financially and so it was natural for her to back him. The publicity centered around her war of words with Dorothy Thompson, who supported the Democratic candidate Franklin D. Roosevelt.
2. In the play the only moderately nice woman was the least interesting, and the entire play did nothing to shed favorable light on women.
3. She was very honest with herself and with others, and her caustic sense of humor and often abrasive tongue caused her many problems with others.
4. She felt like her words were important enough to be covered by the news media. When her demands were met, she advanced the cause of women because the precedent has been followed ever since.
5. There was a great deal of conflict and debate in the Senate before they finally confirmed her appointment. Because of the controversy, Clara Boothe Luce felt it in her own best interests to resign.

DOLLEY MADISON

1. She had been the wife of a Quaker lawyer who died at an early age. She had many friends in Washington, and Madison heard of her through the society grapevine. He asked an acquaintance, Aaron Burr, who was one of her admirers, for an introduction and he knew immediately this was the woman he had waited for. The courtship was very popular among Washington's high society.
2. She got away from the traditional "punch and cake" manner of receiving guests—offering them an entire meal, complemented with her husband's fine wine plus she often had gift lotteries for her guests, and she did it all in grandiose style.

3. He was a scholar and an introvert. She helped boost his ego by restoring his confidence in the decisions he made. She helped him with advice throughout, and her outgoing personality often saved the day and made the administration a popular one.
4. Her tastes were enhanced through her service as official hostess during the Jefferson administration. When her husband became President she already knew what she wanted to do, she was popular in Washington and she was able to do things she felt were necessary.
5. She oftentimes saved her husband by cultivating friendships and associations with wives and daughters of his political enemies. She always seemed to know just whom she should entertain and when. Her timing was another strong suit.

MARGARET MEAD

1. Her mother was a sociologist, and she was also influenced at Bernard College by anthropologists Ruth Benedict and Franz Boas.
2. She felt people can learn to better understand themselves if they learn about other cultures.
3. Simply stated, each generation has a different value system and places emphasis and de-emphasis on different aspects of the culture. Even though generations are often close to each other, they are never in complete accord. That leads to misunderstanding and conflicts, and Mead felt that studying those various cultures could lead to better understanding.
4. Answers will vary but should reflect the constant change going on within all societies, change that needs observation and record keeping.
5. She wrote books and magazine articles, gave speaking presentations, and served on several boards and commissions. She received several honors of merit for her lifelong devotion to the study of other people.

GRANDMA MOSES

1. Because she was 78 years old when she sold her first painting. She painted well into her 80's when her success story began.
2. Christian living, hard work and close family ties ranked high on her list. She also believed in self-sufficiency and having many children—values that were common at that time.
3. She had been taught to be self-sufficient herself and felt that was the way to raise children. Many parents of today are usually more concerned with providing for their children all they can to help them get a head start in life. Also the larger families of her day made the children perhaps more dependent on each other than on their parents.
4. She had always enjoyed painting but had never had time to paint because of the hard working life she lived. Her husband Thomas also had considered it foolish.
5. The entire direction of her busy life was centered around constantly being busy. Her life story is filled with such parallels. What she meant was simply that she could not stand idle time.

SANDRA DAY O'CONNOR

1. She did not like the long rides she had to make just to get to school—and she felt it totally unnecessary to subject students to this merely for the sake of racial equality.
2. In her quest to become a lawyer, she encountered a lot of prejudice and could not get a job with a law firm simply because she was a woman.
3. Reagan had lost the favor of many women during his campaign for the presidency with his opposition to ERA. He was simply trying to mend fences.
4. Reagan meant that her voting record had been fair, that she was intelligent and not prejudiced and that her devotion to public good would serve her well in this high position.
5. Her voting record in the past had indicated she was not against abortion, which was in conflict with conservative Republican values.

JACQUELINE KENNEDY ONASSIS

1. She redecorated with impeccable taste. Reproductions were replaced with original paintings. She had a lot of professional help—but the results were a grand representation of what the executive mansion in a world leader like the United States should be. The furnishings and the decor made it one of the most tastefully done buildings on Earth.
2. Her background, her education and her tastes all suggested first class. She was also the most glamorous of First Ladies. She was also often photographed and her clothes were naturally in the limelight. She looked good in them, thus other people bought the kinds of clothes she bought.
3. Again, her education and cosmopolitan background plus her beauty and natural charm all prepared her for what many Americans enjoyed seeing as their First Lady.
4. The cuisine was supurb, and she was always well-versed on her guests and provided the charm to make their visit a pleasant one. She also had a flair for the extraordinary, relying on historic or extravagant backgrounds and environments to add to the mood.
5. Hers was a glamorous image impression—always seeming to do and say just the right thing. Her husband was a national idol, and the handsome couple created a positive impression that etched itself into the public image, regardless of where they went or what they did, even the way she handled his tragic death.

EMILY POST

1. She grew up amid wealth and fashion and was taught at an early age that which was acceptable and that which was not. Her early exposure to the standards of the day no doubt helped build her confidence in later dictating accepted manners.
2. He was wealthy and accustomed to the same flambuoyant lifestyle of Emily. During her time as a debutante, she had many opportunities to make choices from among her suitors. It seemed she made the right choice until Post lost his money.
3. He represented Funk and Wagnall, a New York publishing house, and he convinced her to write a book on etiquette and good manners. Even though she didn't like the subject, he convinced her there was a need and that she had the talent to do the work.
4. He first told her she was the person for the book. He then quietly left her a copy of the most recent book in print on the subject, and when she read the book she became convinced she could do much better and she went to work.
5. Her background definitely put her in a position to be an authority. However, it was her emphasis on good common sense and high regard for others that made the book catch on with America.

SALLY RIDE

1. Those who were involved in the feminist movement saw her accomplishment as another first for women seeking equality, and they wanted to play up the publicity of her being the first woman.
2. NASA needed qualified scientists to run and interpret its sophisticated equipment and could not compete with the private sector for the high pay commanded by the top scientists in the field.
3. She dropped out of Swarthmore College and worked very hard on her tennis game for three months. At the end of that time, she decided she wasn't good enough to turn professional, so she returned to college.
4. Despite all the symbolism the press attached to the announcement, Crippen denied all reasons other than that she was the best person for the job.
5. Those who were trying to capitalize on Sally Ride's accomplishments were doing so because she was the first woman in space. NASA preferred to play down her being a woman in favor of her being an astronaut.

ELEANOR ROOSEVELT

1. Many thought she was unfeminine, that she interfered in her husband's affairs and that she was undiplomatic in many of the things she said.
2. She overcame the problem through hours of practice and voice lessons. She learned to speak without use of a text and developed the self-confidence that removed the nervous giggle from her presentation.
3. She believed in social equality and did what she could to help black people. She felt that survival of the races depended on learning to live in peace together. Her stand on issues for Blacks made her their hero and they voted Democratic—and still do.
4. In her youth she had been fascinated with the political career of her uncle Theodore Roosevelt, but it was her husband's political advisor, Louis Howe, who influenced her deeply. She also saw an opportunity, when thrust into the limelight, to do something about the issues on which she felt so strongly.
5. She invited her to sing at the White House when Marian Anderson was denied the use of Constitution Hall by the Daughters of the American Revolution, of which Eleanor was a member. She then resigned from the organization and was looked upon as a hero by black people.

DIANA ROSS

1. She always enjoyed singing and sang in the church choir. She also had excellent taste in clothing and design and was even then a classy lady. She also had a burning desire to do well whatever she chose to do.
2. She and two friends, Florence Ballard and Mary Wilson, began by singing on street corners in a group called the Primettes. Their big break came when Berry Gordy introduced them to Motown.
3. He seasoned them as professionals during their time as backup singers; then he changed their name from the Primettes to the Supremes. He then hired a team of songwriters to write songs that were tailored to their style and they became successful.
4. Gold Records are awarded to the artists who have records that sell one million copies.
5. Her versatile singing voice was combined with a self-confidence and stage presence that overwhelmed her audiences.

SACAGAWEA

1. She served as the main guide for the expedition, and her presence assured the Indian groups encountered that their mission was in peace. She also provided food and horses for the group as well as being highly resourceful on many occasions!
2. To find a navigable river that might unite the East Coast with the West Coast
3. Because for about $15 million the United States was able to double its size—a land that contained over 800,000 square miles and would eventually become all or parts of fifteen states
4. The land between the Mississippi and the Rocky Mountains, stretching from the Gulf of Mexico to the Canadian border
5. The woods were teeming with wild game plus the discovery of the Columbia River, the towering mountains, the bountiful forests and the economic potential of the entire area. It also gave the United States control of its waters which was what they wanted in the first place.

BEVERLY SILLS

1. Her parents were convinced of her musical talent and provided her with private lessons when she was very young. She also began study at the age of seven under the tutelage of Estelle Liebling.
2. Her daughter Meredith (Muffy) had a serious loss of hearing and her son Peter was mentally retarded. She was heartbroken over these afflictions and decided to devote herself to their well-being.
3. When she captured the role of Cleopatra in *Julius Caesar,* a role she literally demanded of the New York City Opera, threatening to resign if she didn't get the role
4. Her long career has many highlights, but becoming the director of the New York Opera is something she longed for for many years.
5. She was extremely proud of her achievements in opera despite the fact that she could be successful without appearing at the Metropolitan Opera and without first establishing herself as a star in Europe.

MARGARET CHASE SMITH

1. Her husband, Clyde, was a member of Congress when he had a heart attack. His doctor urged Margaret to finish his term. She accepted the challenge of finishing his term, and he died soon after of another attack.

2. She would applaud her efforts, even though Ferraro was a Democrat. Smith herself ran unsuccessfully for the presidency; and even though she gained only a few votes, she was respected for her efforts.
3. She had a strong sense of conviction and an overpowering devotion to her public duty.
4. She cited case after case of inconsistency even reversal between what Kennedy said he stood for during the campaign of 1960 and how he actually performed as President.
5. She strongly supported the American right to criticize, to protest and to support unpopular beliefs, and she was outraged at the totalitarian tactics of McCarthy, which she said would spell the end of the American way of life.

GLORIA STEINEM

1. Answers will vary, but she no doubt felt a strong passion to succeed and felt that the barriers held up against women prevented them from gaining what they rightfully deserved.
2. To encourage women to seek political office and work for legislation that will advance the rights of women
3. She felt women needed a national forum from which to speak for themselves. Most magazines for women were both owned and controlled by men. Steinem wanted a magazine completely controlled by women.
4. Her heartbeats speeded up and her mouth went dry. She became obsessed with getting to the end of a sentence before swallowing—then would regret later not saying what she wished she had.
5. She went to Canada where she was unknown. There she did a TV series that could be edited before airing. She also consulted a speech teacher and would sometimes pretend she was Eleanor Roosevelt. She was so very dedicated to her cause that she became determined to overcome her problem at any cost.

LUCY STONE

1. She rejected the biblical stand on men ruling over women. She felt it was a male-dominated marriage if the man's last name was used. So she kept her own name. She also had the word *obey* omitted from the marriage vows.
2. Elizabeth Cady Stanton, Susan B. Anthony, Antoinette Brown
3. Nette was studying to become a minister, and she could see a lot of good coming from the family unit in its biblical sense. Lucy feared that her friend Nette would become enslaved by marriage.
4. She would have given her whole-hearted support and would have felt it was a step in the right direction toward making a woman President.
5. Answers will vary, but her ideas would revolve around self-sufficiency and independence, and she would encourage her daughter to never allow herself to be dominated by a man.

HARRIET BEECHER STOWE

1. His constant regard for the good of mankind no doubt had an influence on her strong feelings of reform.
2. She felt a peace and calm that she had never experienced with her directive husband, and she enjoyed it so much she parlayed it out longer than needed. It no doubt taught her husband a lesson as well.
3. It was so overwhelmingly popular that Harriet continued to add chapters.
4. Her book formulated a national feeling on the wrong of slavery, and it was so widely read that it became a point of focus among those who wanted to abolish slavery.
5. With her sister Catherine Beecher, she wrote a manual for women on how to run a household. In the book, they constantly made reference to the importance of the woman and what her role should be.

BARBRA STREISAND

1. Her father was well-educated and his family was on the rise financially. When he died, he left his family without adequate funds. Barbra Streisand has said she doubts she would have become the fighter she is had her father lived and provided her with the comforts she desired.
2. Charisma is that rare quality held only by a few people. It's almost like a power over others that combines charm with grace and popularity and respect and attractiveness that makes people admire the individual very much.
3. She disregarded fashion and design and created an offbeat image that could not be ignored. It caught on and was soon copied by others.
4. She did indeed have something of an ego problem; however, she preferred to say it was her strive for perfection that caused her to want things her own way.
5. *Funny Girl*
Hello Dolly!
The Way We Were
The Owl and the Pussycat
A Star Is Born
On a Clear Day You Can See Forever

HARRIET TUBMAN

1. Moses. They paralleled her efforts of leading them to freedom in Canada to the biblical figure who led the Jews out of Egypt.
2. It was her total devotion to the cause. Great people who make these kinds of commitments are so dedicated to their causes, they don't worry about their own personal safety.
3. Obviously travel at night would be safer. Also they had no maps, and many followed the big dipper with the North Star being their guiding light.
4. When she was a little girl, she tried to help a slave who was being punished. The white overseer was so angry he fractured her skull.
5. Accept any reasonable answers that suggest she would probably be happy but would continue to work for even better conditions.

BARBARA WALTERS

1. Her father was a nightclub owner in New York City, and Barbara was exposed to celebrities at an early age. She was thus not awed by them when it became her job to interview them.
2. She had worked behind the scenes as a writer for several years, but NBC policy would not allow her the top job because she wasn't a "recognized" name. When actress Maureen O'Sullivan abruptly quit, they allowed her the job "on a trial basis" and she was immediately accepted.
3. She was intelligent and she asked probing questions in her interviews. She had, after all, years of experience behind the scenes and she always did her homework—making the interviews more successful and significant.
4. She claims she has the ability to make those she interviews feel comfortable and more willing to answer her often pointed questions.
5. While she supports many of the issues women are fighting for, she still prefers most of the traditional roles reserved for women.

MARTHA WASHINGTON

1. Her husband had been in the limelight during the struggle for independence. Once that was attained, she was hoping to spend happy days at Mount Vernon with George.
2. Socially, she felt it was far below both Williamsburg and Philadelphia. But she did go about dignifying her position as First Lady—accepting guests and entertaining as she was supposed to do.
3. She was the daughter of a Virginia squire and had learned much in the way of social grace. She was indeed a fashionable young lady and refined in music, dancing, conversation and proper etiquette of the day.
4. She was totally devoted to both—helping to tend to the sick and wounded. She brought supplies and copied important papers—doing whatever George asked her to do. She also helped stifle rumors and bring comfort and cheer to the soldiers during bleak times.
5. Martha's son Jacky, by her first marriage, insisted on seeing the surrender, but he contracted camp fever and eventually died.

FRANCES WILLARD

1. They were against the use of alcohol and the hardships that resulted from its abuse. But the Union was also against drug abuse and advocated labor reform as well as advanced the causes of peace and woman suffrage.

2. The atmosphere in the United States was one of carefree living and reckless abandon. People did not like being told what to do and balked at the government banning the sale of alcohol. The result was crime and violence that was associated with the illegal brewing, sale and consumption of alcohol that was often impure and sometimes caused death. The government finally had enough and wrote the idea off as a failure by repealing the 18th Amendment.

3. Under the plan she proposed thirty-nine activities that would improve the status of women. There were welfare programs, peace programs, welfare work for prisons and equalization ideas to help minorities and even police matrons who would help to ensure that the right principles for living were taught to the young.

4. Men considered their attacks on the saloon attacks on their masculinity. The fact that they were so well-organized was also a threat to men, and the result was a hostility vented against women in general, but more particularly against all the W.C.T.U. represented.

5. She had remarkable tact and persuasive ability. She was also persistent and refused to accept defeat. Her very presence carried with it an air of excitement, and she was beloved by thousands. She was one of the most powerful women in the United States at the time, but would not have been so without the personality she possessed.

BABE DIDRIKSON ZAHARIAS

1. She was quoted in an ad for Dodge cars which was interpreted as an endorsement. She didn't really do this and was totally innocent but was ruled a professional anyway.

2. Amateur rules were very different then than now, and they weren't allowed to take anything. Even as a professional, there weren't enough tournaments for women to make a good living.

3. An amateur by definition is one who plays a sport purely for the love of the sport. A professional plays for money. In recent years, some of the rules have been somewhat changed to allow amateur athletes to restore at least some of their expenses and still keep their amateur standing.

4. She had to write a letter to Joe Dey, executive secretary of USGA, applying for readmission as an amateur. She also needed four letters of endorsement from leading amateurs, and then she had to drop all professional contracts for three tours. She applied in January of 1940 and was reinstated in January of 1943.

5. Prior to the LPGA tour, there were only about two tournaments per year for women who were professional golfers.